REMARKABLE!
Resolving your most important business issue.

ROSS ✦ SALYERS

"Indeed, true transformation begins on the inside before it's revealed on the outside. This book is a catalyst for personal and cultural transformation."

—**Orrin Woodward**
New York Times Best-Selling Author & Founder of
LIFE Leadership Company

"If fate has brought this book to your attention - you need to read it. My MBA professor once told me that the best professors don't just teach you - they teach you how to think. Reading ***Remarkable!*** makes you feel like you're a fly on the wall, listening to the most important conversation about life and business that you never heard."

—**Rick Schirmer**
Founder & CEO PartnersHub
(former brand strategy executive, The Walt Disney Company)

"***Remarkable!*** is onto the powerful idea of organizing our businesses and our lives around the pursuit of values. It is not enough to know the "what" and the "how." If we understand and embrace the "why," it changes everything."

—**Dave Stockert**
CEO, Post Properties

"This book is a virtual cornucopia of ideas that will help build a culture replete with enthusiasm, productivity and widespread self-assessment - all leading to very high levels of individual and collective performance."

—**Stan Richards**
Founder and Principal, The Richards Group

"*Remarkable!* takes competent scholarship, a wealth of practical experience, and solid good sense, and then adds an ingredient that is so often missing in most professional presentations--the ability to communicate in an interesting, intriguing, and engaging manner. It addresses topics and areas of essential concern to modern organizations in ways that leap beyond the sterile approaches so often seen today."

—STEVE BYRUM, PHD.
President, Judgment Index
& Past President, Robert S. Hartman Institute

"*Remarkable!* is a clear and practical presentation of a transformational process guaranteed to change you personally and professionally. As you will read, it is up to you to take ownership and responsibility for the change you desire. *Remarkable!* shows you how to do just that."

—KEVIN EDMONDS
Senior Director of Talent, Performance & Development,
The Kroger Company

"The Theories of Value Creation are both complex and impactful. *Remarkable!* explains value creation in terms that anyone can understand and apply to life and business with profoundly positive results."

—JOEL MANBY
President and CEO, Herschend Family Entertainment

"The challenge of choice is woven into the fabric of our lives. *Remarkable!* describes clearly how our choices define us and provide a path to create value for the people we touch. It is undoubtedly one of the best life lesson books I have read."

—ROBERT J. CERONE
CEO, Laurus Strategies

"In the battle of skill versus will, great leaders demonstrate a unique ability to focus on things that produce positive results. As Randy and David lay out in this wonderful parable, we are all designed to add value to the people around us. If you consciously make the decision to promote and put into practice the truths in **Remarkable!**, then optimal results are sure to follow."

—Tommy Newberry
New York Times Best-Selling Author of *The 4:8 Principle*

"Although everything in life *IS* a choice, reading **Remarkable!** should not be. This book is as applicable to your personal life as it is to your professional life. I highly encourage readers to choose to invest the time to glean the principles taught within its pages. You won't regret it."

—Tash Elwyn
President, Private Client Group,
Raymond James & Associates, Inc.

"Clear, compelling, and inspiring… if you need anything else to motivate you to read this book, it is simply transformational!"

—Todd Duncan
New York Times Best-Selling Author of
Time Traps: Proven Strategies for Swamped Salespeople and
High Trust Selling: Make More Money in Less Time with Less Stress

"The concepts presented in **Remarkable!** are clear, concise and compelling. Apply them and they have the power to transform your life and business for the better."

—David Seibert
Director of Business Development, LifeWay

"Dr. Randy Ross and David Salyers do a brilliant job connecting familiar processes (like how a clutch works in a car) with a simple, yet profound explanation of how these same processes can be applied to build a business, hire the right staff, create customer loyalty and measure success from a fresh perspective. The story format is entertaining to read and makes it easy to remember the principles. Get two highlighters to read this book. I needed one color for ideas to implement personally, and the second was to make it easy to revisit the great training ideas!"

—MICHELE SHODA VELCHECK
Founder of Solid Source Realty

"This is a counterintuitive approach to business that will move any organization toward **Remarkable!** More importantly, it isn't limited to organizational life. The principles within this book can extend deeply into our personal lives, and that's great news. After all, don't we all want a Remarkable life?"

—JEFF HENDERSON
Lead Pastor, Gwinnett Church

"There are plenty of sales-related books that describe tactics and strategies to win more business. I've yet to find a book like **Remarkable!** that helps sales professionals understand the principles of personal effectiveness with their clients and prospects. This book will be a game-changer for sales teams that recognize that the best product doesn't win most of the time!"

—PETER BOURKE
Principal of The Complex Sale & Author of the best-selling eBook, *UnSelling™: 22 Strategies to Win Without Selling*

"In life and business there are those who position themselves to extract value from every endeavor, and others who attempt to create and bring value to every encounter. *Remarkable!* clearly teaches everyone how to do the latter. If you want a book that can help you transform your corporate culture, this is it!"

—CHRISTOPHER C. COLLIER
Director, HR, Southern Company

"*Remarkable!* takes the entire philosophy behind associate engagement to the next level. As leaders we are required to create a positive work environment where people have the opportunity to express giftedness and achieve something greater than self. But this takes the next step. Instead of just putting the onus of engagement on the employer, *Remarkable!* suggests that the associate must then make a choice to engage and contribute to the organization and its mission. Only then can both the employer and the employee fully realize their potential. This is an easy-to-read, very powerful message."

—SCOTT MACLELLAN
CEO, TouchPoint Support Services

"Being *Remarkable!* is really a choice – a commitment to making things better for others. This book will inspire and challenge you as you create a road map for yourself, your team and your organization. A must read for the intentional leader."

—JEREMIE KUBICEK
Founder of GiANT Impact and author of the National Best-Seller, *Making Your Leadership Come Alive.*

"Randy Ross and David Salyers have hit the nail on the head with this book. They actually model what they teach and what they embody is what I wish college graduates all over the world could understand—that finding the right job means adding value, not extracting it from an organization. May this book spread like wildfire."

—TIM ELMORE
Author and President of GrowingLeaders.com

"Live on purpose – with a purpose. *Remarkable!* will become mandatory reading for all Stafford School of Business students and faculty, as it is the road map to making a positive difference in people's lives."

—MARK "DILL" DRISCOLL
Founder, World Sports Promotion, Momentum, ignition
& Dean, Stafford School of Business at
Abraham Baldwin Agricultural College

Remarkable!
©2013 by Randy Ross and David Salyers.
All rights reserved.
Published by Enthusiasm, Inc., Atlanta, GA

NOTE: This is a fictional story with fictional characters and entities, with one noted exception. *Robert S. Hartman*, known to many as the modern father of axiology, was a well-known and highly respected philosopher, educator, scientist and business consultant. For more information on Robert S. Hartman, please refer to the tribute in the appendix.

All rights reserved. No part of this publication may be reproduced, stored in a retrieval system, or transmitted in any form or by any means – electronic, mechanical, photocopy, recording, or any other – except for brief quotations in printed reviews, without the prior permission of the publisher.

The scanning, uploading, and distribution of this book via the Internet or via any other means without the permission of the publisher is illegal and punishable by law. Please purchase only authorized electronic editions and do not participate in or encourage electronic piracy of copyrightable materials. Your support of the author's rights is appreciated.

ISBN: 978-0-9882184-1-3
LCCN: 2012923778
Cover & interior design: Pat Malone
Printed in the United States of America

REMARKABLE!

*is dedicated to the most Remarkable! people in our lives:
LuAnne and Lynn for their unconditional love and support.
And to Ryan, Lindsay and Colton – as well as Amanda, Nick and
Daniel, whose futures we hope will be brightened
by the application of these truths.*

Contents

Foreword   xii
Introduction   xiv

SECTION ONE: Assessment

    1. Shifting Gears   1
    2. The Clutch   7
    3. Tune-Up   17
    4. The Oil Change   27

SECTION TWO: Alignment

    5. Valucentricity   45
    6. On Purpose   55
    7. Creativity   61
    8. Positivity   71

SECTION THREE: Adjustment

    9. Sustainability   81
    10. Choice   91
    11. Responsibility   113
    12. The Question   123

SECTION FOUR: Advancement

    13. Transformation   137
    14. Resistance   149
    15. Remarkable   157
    16. Reward   177

Appendices

Appendix A: How to Use Remarkable   190

Appendix B: Assess Yourself   192

Appendix C: Remarkable Culture Survey   194

Appendix D: Tribute to Robert S. Hartman   196

Appendix E: Glossary of Terms   198

Appendix F: Maxims of Value Creation   200

Bibliography   *202*

Acknowledgements   *204*

About the Authors   *206*

Foreword

I have always believed that a good name is more desirable than great riches. While profits are important in any business, maintaining a strong sense of values and living out your convictions are imperative. If a company's good name to the outside world is its brand, then its real character is revealed in its culture. And while there is much discussion about the need to create a compelling corporate culture in the marketplace today, very few understand the dynamics at play and how to address them effectively. Taking simple truths and placing them in a corporate parable, ***Remarkable!*** provides the reader with both an enjoyable format and transformational insights.

I am convinced that if you help others get what they want, you will eventually get what you want. A deep love for people causes you to focus your efforts on providing the best for them rather than constantly thinking about what you want to receive from them. This simple concept transforms relationships and the work experience and is at the core of good business.

The truths contained within the pages of what you are about to read are a clear and succinct articulation of the principles which create the superior advantage in business. If embraced and applied, these principles can have a profoundly positive impact on the culture of any company. At the same time, they have the power to enhance your professional life. But please don't stop there. Apply them to your personal life and watch them transform your closest relationships as well. After all, there is no better way to invest your time and energy than in strengthening relationships. It truly is My Pleasure to encourage you to read and apply the truths contained within the pages of *Remarkable!*

S. Truett Cathy
Founder & CEO, Chick-fil-A, Inc.

Introduction

There are millions of businesses and organizations, but only a handful of them could be described as **Remarkable!** Have you ever wondered why? Remarkable means notably or conspicuously unusual; extraordinary; worthy of notice or attention. The ideas explored in this book have come from a lifetime of observing some extraordinary people and organizations as they live out their conspicuously unusual ideas, producing uncommon results. The effect is that those who work for, and those who benefit from, these people and organizations find themselves with an irrepressible desire to "remark about them!" What is it that these folks know that others seemingly do not? How does their view of the world lead them to think and behave differently than others? When faced with the same opportunities and challenges, how are their choices different…and why?

Remarkable! is an attempt to answer these questions and resolve the most important issue facing businesses today. Once you understand the basic premise and apply the principles contained within these pages, then a transformation is almost certain. We encourage you to begin a revolution that will infuse new life and energy into your organization and help people find significance and fulfillment in their work.

Life is either limited or enhanced by your choices. Leadership is about influencing people to make conspicuously unusual choices that bring health and happiness to life and work. The choices you make will eventually make you. We challenge you to choose to be **Remarkable!**

The Authors

"Nothing is so common-place as to wish to be remarkable."

Oliver Wendell Holmes, Sr.
The Autocrat of the Breakfast Table (1858), Ch. XII

SECTION ONE
ASSESSMENT

Chapter One

Shifting Gears

The tires thumped a syncopated rhythm in time with the joints in the pavement of the flyover just north of Midtown. The driver's mind was spinning as quickly as the wheels on his candy apple red 1968 Thunderbird convertible. An innocent indulgence that he had afforded himself shortly after his thirty-ninth birthday, the classic car was a mid-life purchase that brought much joy. It rolled off the assembly line the very month of his birth, and he had always been drawn to the sheer power and sleek elegance of this particular automobile of that bygone era. He took great pride in keeping it in mint condition and enjoyed the attention that he received when he occasionally took it on road trips to the beach. Though he rarely drove the car to work, today he was glad he had. With the top down and the sun out, it was pure therapy. This commute home was actually welcomed, giving him time to reflect upon everything that had happened that week at work.

Dusty Harts was the Vice President of Query, a customer care service provider in the utilities industry. Based in Atlanta, Dusty was responsible for giving oversight to their three call centers in the Southeast. With over eight hundred energy advisors in his chain of command, the demands of life as the leader of such a heavily customer-facing operation were formidable. To add to the burden, results of Query's recent Employee Engagement Survey had come in two weeks earlier and the scores could be referred to generously as "not good."

For two years, Dusty had found comfort in the fact that employee turnover was at an all-time low. He was optimistic that somehow the company had finally slowed the spin of the revolving back door that previously churned associates through the organization. Now, it appeared, the bubble had burst. He knew that economic winds were adverse and few companies were hiring in the market. This reality kept the issues hidden by limiting options for the disgruntled and disillusioned. In spite of the fact that his teams were meeting client expectations, morale was a topic of constant concern. His gut told him that things were not all good, but he never expected such an abrupt reality check. The Employee Engagement Survey painted a picture of unhappy, unmotivated teams, with a significant number of employees seemingly slogging through the drudgery of their daily activities. By their responses, many team members had indicated that they were experiencing little satisfaction or fulfillment in their current environments. The findings from the survey had sent leaders throughout the organization into a frenzied tailspin.

Employee engagement had become a critical metric for Query ever since Gallup, a leading research organization, had published studies definitively linking higher levels of engagement to higher productivity. Leaders knew, intuitively, that the employee experience and the customer experience were inseparably linked, but this research had actually quantified the connection. If an employee was unhappy in her role and brought little enthusiasm to the work experience, a lackluster attitude would most certainly carry over into the customer encounter.

On the other hand, it had also been firmly established that the higher the emotional attachment to one's work, the more passionate and productive the performance. Measuring, monitoring and moving engagement levels in a positive direction could produce profound results. Therefore, engagement was at the heart of what Query called their *Transformational Triad*. This three-pronged mission statement encapsulated their commitment to engagement. It simply read, *"Engage, Empower and Enrich the Life of Every Associate and Customer."* It sounded impressive and it was certainly visible on plaques and posters throughout the building. It was displayed prominently in the lobby, alongside the vision and values statements. The real challenge was in trying to figure out how to add some walk to the talk. Dusty often wondered how many of his team members could recite these statements, let alone explain them or embody them.

Once the survey results reached the leadership team, Jim Mitchell, the CFO of Query, had formed a task force to address the troublesome findings. The stated objective of this elite ad hoc team was to determine a course of action that would turn the tide and reverse the downward trending. And Dusty had been tapped to be a part of the task force. He wanted to believe that Jim placed great confidence in his judgment and valued him as a key player in the transformation process. After all, Jim was influential in hiring Dusty six years ago. Since that time, Jim had served as a confidant and mentor. He was one of Dusty's biggest cheerleaders.

On the other hand, Dusty's teams were among those that scored poorly on the survey. He wondered if his reputation as a leader had been tarnished by the less than stellar report. At some level, he thought, it would be taken as a reflection of his leadership. Either way, it threw him into the proverbial lion's den, staring into the teeth of what was sure to be a season of long hours and countless meetings as they attempted to determine what was causing their corporate sails to luff in the wind.

Dusty was trying not to let the whirlwind in his head prevent him from enjoying the beginning of a beautiful spring weekend. Pushing the tense internal conversation to the back of his mind, he approached the exit that would take him to his well-manicured community in the suburbs of North Atlanta. As he approached the turn and depressed the clutch, he struggled to get the car into a lower gear. He had experienced difficulties in shifting the last few times he had driven his "ball of fire," as he affectionately called it. This time the grinding was unnerving, signaling it was time to have someone look at what might be malfunctioning. And he knew just where to take it to get an assessment. Having left the office a little early, he decided to run by Classic Car Care, where he had developed a good relationship with the owner. If he could get there by six o'clock, someone might be able to take a look and, if needed, get the work done the following day. That way, he reasoned, he could have it back in time to drive it to church on Sunday morning, which was something he loved to do when the weather permitted.

Dusty pulled up to Classic Car Care right at six o'clock, fearing that he may have missed his window of opportunity. He fully expected that he would have to come back again the next morning. But true to form, the owner, Fred, came sauntering out to greet him.

Fred Walters always made Dusty feel like they were the best of friends, even though the only time he ever saw Fred was when he brought the family vehicles in for routine maintenance. Fred was a stately gentleman in his mid-sixties, with a tall frame and wavy gray hair. He was unusually fit for a man his age and always neatly dressed. Dusty often thought it odd that his khaki pants and shirt were perfectly pressed even if soiled by oil and grime from the shop. Half the time, Fred could be seen out front with customers, and the other half he would be working diligently on someone's car in one of the bays. In either place, Fred always seemed to be remarkably at ease and comfortable whether he was working with a wrench in his hand or on the phone, talking with a customer.

"Hey, Dusty, what brings you our way on a beautiful day like today?" Fred asked with his usual Cheshire cat grin that could light up any room.

By the warm greeting and light tone in his voice, you would have thought Fred had all the time in the world to talk with Dusty.

"I've been having difficulty shifting gears, and I was wondering if you could take a look and see what's going on. I think the clutch is going out," said Dusty.

"We're closing for the night. If you'll pull her into the second bay, I'll give her a once over first thing in the morning and give you a call. Does that work for you?" Fred asked.

"That would be great," Dusty responded. "I'll call my son, Mike, and have him come pick me up."

"Don't bother. I can drop you off on my way home," Fred offered. "I can run you to your house and still get cleaned up in time to take Anne out for our date tonight. Come on."

Agreeing to Fred's offer, Dusty pulled the T-bird into the bay while Fred gave a few last instructions to his partner in the front office. Then, the two men climbed into Fred's restored vintage 1948 pickup and drove away chatting about their love of classic cars like two giddy teenage girls talking about boys.

Chapter Two

The Clutch

Dusty's cell phone rang shortly after nine o'clock the following morning. It was Fred calling from Classic Car Care.

"You were right," he said to Dusty. "The clutch has gone out and needs to be replaced. I can get the parts and have it ready for you by the end of the day, if you like."

"Perfect," Dusty responded. "I'll swing by late this afternoon to pick it up."

Shortly after four o'clock, Dusty's 17-year-old son dropped him off at Classic. His T-bird was sitting in the parking lot, washed and ready to go. Standard operating procedure at Classic was to take all the cars next door to the car wash for final prep before returning them to their owners. It was a nice touch and clients appreciated it.

Dusty walked into the waiting area. He could see Fred talking with someone in his office. When Fred saw Dusty, he waved and said he would be with him in a few minutes. The day was winding down and the only other person on the premises was one of the mechanics cleaning up the shop. Dusty took a seat in one of the comfortable leather chairs and picked up the current copy of the *Harvard Business Review* off the coffee table. It struck him as a bit strange that Fred would be receiving *HBR* at the shop, but it was a fleeting thought. He quickly became engrossed in an article entitled, "Managing Yourself: The Paradox of Excellence." He couldn't hear the conversation through the open doorway, but it was punctuated by laughter, which occasionally distracted him from his reading.

After awhile, Fred walked out of his office and said, "Hey Dusty, I want you to meet an old friend of mine. This is Howard Levine. Howard and I go back to college days when we used to compete for the attention of the same girls. He dropped by today in search of sage advice and business counsel," Fred quipped in a tongue-in-cheek sort of way.

"It's a pleasure to meet you, Dusty," said Howard. "Fred was showing me your car earlier. It's a beauty!" Dusty was a bit taken aback. He knew Howard Levine by reputation. As one of the most widely respected business leaders in the Southeast, he had taken the helm of two Fortune 500 companies that were headed for the rocks and turned them around. In both situations, he steered them clear of disaster, brought them through rough waters, and made them profitable against significant odds. He was lauded by many as the Master of Business Transformation.

"Thank you," Dusty stammered. "Fred helps me keep it in good running condition. And, it's a pleasure to meet you as well."

"Well, I best be on my way. I've mined what little knowledge Fred has left and I've taken the last nuggets of gold," Howard taunted.

"Don't pay any attention to him," Fred interjected. "He's still jealous that I married the only girl he couldn't get a date with during college. Her standards were much too high."

With that good-natured barb still in his side, Howard laughed and hugged Fred before he disappeared out the door. "Come on into my office, if you have the time," Fred offered.

"Sure," Dusty said, accepting the invitation.

Though overwhelmed by the fact that he had just met Howard Levine, Dusty tried to maintain a sense of composure. He had never been in Fred's office. It was modest but nicely appointed, with pictures of family and friends from trips and special occasions adorning the majority of shelves and wall space. Rather than sitting behind his desk, Fred gestured toward a table in the corner and offered Dusty a chair. While Dusty was taking his seat, Fred reached into the closet and retrieved two bottles of water from a small refrigerator. Dusty could contain his curiosity no longer. As Fred handed him a bottle, he started blurting out questions.

"Did you really go to school with Howard Levine? Didn't he graduate from Harvard?"

"Drug him through is more accurate," Fred laughed. "We were roommates for two years. I'm still not sure how either one of us made it through the MBA program. He was constantly distracted by living life large and I was too serious for both of us."

"You graduated from the Harvard Business School?"

"Surprised?" Fred asked. "I haven't always owned this shop. Tinkering with cars is a passion that I always wanted to turn into a business. I guess you could say that I am just enjoying my retirement. I was lucky enough to figure out a way to get people to pay me to do what I enjoy – working on cars. I like to fix things and get them running smoothly."

For a moment, Dusty sat in stunned silence as the reality sank in. The guy who just fixed his car was a graduate of Harvard, and he was Howard Levine's roommate. "So, he *really was* seeking business advice from you?"

"Not really," Fred said. "We just miss the banter of the old days and sometimes enjoy popping in on one another to kick a few ideas around. He was on this side of town and decided to swing by and wish me a happy anniversary. As of yesterday, Anne and I have been married for forty-two years. And yes, it is a fact that he never did get a date with her. But that is enough about me. I wanted to ask you about something that came up in our conversation last night as I was driving you home."

"Sure, what was that?" Dusty asked.

"Actually, it wasn't so much what you said as it was what you didn't say. When I asked you how work was going, your answer was vague and evasive. Not at all the response that I would expect from someone who was enjoying his work," Fred observed.

His comment was pointed but not the least bit offensive. When Fred asked about his work the night before, Dusty had taken the question as small talk and brushed it off. Now he realized that Fred was genuinely interested.

"Is everything all right at work?" Fred asked.

"To be honest," Dusty answered, "things at work are a bit tense. Life in a call center environment is hard enough. Now, our engagement scores have come back at an all-time low, and everyone is in a panic to figure out what is wrong and what corrective actions might be taken to turn things around. Just when I thought things were sailing along smoothly, I get hit by this squall!"

"I could tell that something was bothering you. Now it all makes sense," Fred said. "But, let me ask you something. What made you think things were going smoothly?"

"Well, our attrition rates have been good and we were hitting our numbers," Dusty responded.

"But through the survey your people are telling you that they aren't happy with their current work situation, which means lost opportunities, lackluster customer support, and a significant number of people who have already emotionally disengaged and are only staying for a paycheck," offered Fred.

Dusty wasn't sure if that was a question or an observation. Either way, it was astute.

"Sounds to me like you are having a problem with your

clutch," Fred suggested.

Now Dusty was really confused. He wondered why Fred was changing the course of the conversation back to his car.

"I thought you said that you fixed the clutch?"

"On your T-bird, I did. But I am referring to your work. The clutch, as you well know, provides the linkage between the engine and the transmission, which ultimately provides power to the drive shaft. When the clutch is engaged, the power produced by the engine is harnessed and transferred to the drive shaft to produce motion. If the clutch is disengaged, then the engine continues to produce power, but it is uncoupled from the drive shaft, rendering it incapable of turning the wheels and garnering traction. You literally cannot 'get things into gear' when the clutch is malfunctioning. As I said, you have a clutch problem – at work!

"The condition of the clutch determines how much discretionary effort your people are willing to put forth. It reflects the level of loyalty, passion and enthusiasm your team members bring to the endeavor. In the final analysis, the clutch will determine momentum and levels of performance."

Dusty was rendered speechless. What a great analogy of engagement, he thought. He wanted to understand more fully what Fred meant. So, he asked him a clarifying question.

"What exactly do you mean by 'the clutch?'"

"The clutch," Fred said, "is the mechanism that provides for the engagement of two or more components to produce motion. On an interpersonal level, a clutch situation is any encounter that requires the engagement of two or more people to create progress – which is just about every human interaction. A clutch situation could be a challenge, a setback, a new directive or a vast opportunity that calls your team to step it up. It could be anything that rocks the status quo or it could be something as simple as a conversation between colleagues. Any situation that requires two or more parties to work together is a clutch situation.

A clutch situation is any encounter that requires the engagement of two or more people to create progress.

"As you know, 'clutch player' is a term often used in sports. It refers to a player who responds with stellar performance in the heat of the moment, when the pressure is high. A clutch player has the emotional constitution of a winner. Clutch players become evident in times of challenge and transition. In the clutch, a person will either step up to the plate or withdraw into the safety of the shadows. When the game is on the line, a clutch player always wants the ball! So, if you have an engagement problem, you have a clutch problem."

"So what do you do about it?" asked Dusty.

"You fix it - just like I did on your T-bird," Fred said matter-of-factly.

"All right, but how do you do that?" Dusty asked as he leaned forward in his chair.

"Now that's a conversation for another day," Fred responded. "Anne and I have some more celebrating to do this weekend and it's time for me to get home. But, if you have any interest, I would be willing to continue the conversation at a later date." With that offer hanging in the air, Fred escorted Dusty to the waiting area where he gave him his paperwork and keys before ushering him to the front door.

"Enjoy the rest of your weekend," Fred said to Dusty.

Almost as quickly as he could utter, "Thanks, you too," Dusty found himself standing outside of Classic Car Care. He wasn't sure what had just happened. He was stunned. He felt like a quarterback who had just been blindsided in the pocket. He came to pick up his car and was floored by insights about his business – offered up by his mechanic – who had completed graduate school at Harvard. Dusty made a conscious effort not to look dazed and confused as he slowly walked to his car.

After driving home, Dusty went straight to his computer and did a search on Fred Walters. What he discovered was impressive. Eight years earlier, Fred had been the CEO of Performax, a thriving multinational software company. Performax had been listed as one of the *Best Places to Work* the last five years that Fred led the company. They had also been repeatedly recognized by the *Business Chronicle* as a leader in Cultural Transformation. Dusty couldn't believe what he was reading. And he couldn't wait to call Classic Car Care again on Monday to schedule a time to have the oil changed in his wife's car – whether it needed it or not.

✦

CHAPTER THREE

Tune-Up

Dusty was in the office early Monday morning to prepare for meetings that started at eight o'clock. Shortly after ten thirty, he was back at his desk dialing the number for Classic Car Care.

"May I speak with Fred, please?"

The person on the other end of the phone line answered, "He's not here today. He usually comes in on Tuesdays, Thursdays and Fridays. May I help you?"

"I wanted to schedule a time for an oil change," Dusty said.

"I can help you with that. When would you like to come in?"

"Whenever Fred is around and you're not too busy," Dusty blurted out before he realized how silly it sounded. "What I mean is, well, I would really like to spend some time talking with Fred, if that is possible, while the oil is being changed," Dusty stammered.

"When would you suggest I come in?"

"Actually, you aren't the first person to ask that question. Right now, it looks like he might have some time on Thursday afternoon. Why don't we schedule you to come in around four o'clock, and I'll ask him to hold the hour for you. How would that work?"

"That would be great. Thanks so much. I will see you Thursday at four o'clock," Dusty confirmed.

The rest of the day was a blur. After asking his administrative assistant, Tara, to clear his calendar beyond three o'clock on Thursday afternoon, he went straight into two phone conferences, a lunch meeting with his team leaders that ran until mid-afternoon, and then a meeting with members of the IT team to troubleshoot a technical problem. By late afternoon, he was back at his desk ready to prep for his meeting the next morning with the Employee Engagement Task Force.

Dusty reached into his files and retrieved a copy of the latest Employee Engagement Survey Report. He also gathered all of the research and notes he had compiled over the years that might be relevant to the topic. He reviewed the reports from the previous two Employee Engagement Surveys and saw the obvious downward trending. He then perused his notes from the focus groups, which had been conducted shortly after the results were reported from the last two surveys. He also reviewed the list of action items that had been crafted by leadership to address the areas that "needed development." And last but not least, he examined the implementation notes on the fulfillment of each corrective initiative across the organization.

After dissecting the reports for more than an hour, Dusty was growing frustrated. He began to question why the multiple corporate initiatives had garnered such meager results. In some instances, they had absolutely no positive impact whatsoever. It just didn't make sense. It seemed illogical that they had spent all that time, energy, and resources to create massive initiatives to address what seemingly were areas of concern for their associates and then to fail to move the needle of engagement northward. Dusty couldn't help but wonder why their corporate compass was so badly broken.

Dusty had personally spearheaded two of those initiatives, in conjunction with other leaders in the organization. One of the initiatives was still a source of deep frustration for him. It addressed educational opportunities within the organization, or supposedly the lack thereof. One of the areas in which the scores had been comparatively low was related to questions on the survey about whether or not there were "sufficient opportunities for team members to learn and grow." In the subsequent focus groups, it became obvious that employees were not asking for more job-related developmental opportunities. What eventually became clear was that associates wanted the opportunity to grow in life-management skills – the "soft stuff," as Dusty often called it. Specific topics suggested were related to effectively dealing with personal finances, time management and improving communication.

In response, a series of workshops were crafted to address those specific topics, and they were offered on a quarterly basis. Time and resources had been allocated to bring in some highly qualified and highly paid presenters. Attendance was purely voluntary. After nine months, the workshops were abandoned because of lack of attendance.

What really never made much sense to Dusty was why the organization would be expected to fill a void that should have been addressed in the home or in school. If someone was having trouble managing their finances, should the company really be expected to help them develop a personal budget? Beyond that, some of the questions on the survey related to aspects of individual socialization that Dusty was certain that the organization could do little about. One particular question - or a variation of it - that consistently came up on the surveys really got under Dusty's skin. That question was, "Do you have a best friend at work?" The question itself was strange to Dusty. He understood that working in an environment where you considered some of your colleagues to be your friends was good for morale. But what if someone didn't have a BFF at work? Was it the manager's responsibility to appoint a best friend to every employee? The thought itself made Dusty chuckle under his breath. The humor of it broke the tension that he was feeling, if only momentarily.

He mused over the fact that so many team leaders throughout the organization had become frustrated by the fact that, in spite of a lack of clarity, they were tasked with identifying corrective measures. Consequently, the "remedies" often quickly degenerated into nothing more than organizing bowling outings and pizza parties in a feeble attempt to boost morale. There was a growing knot in the pit of Dusty's stomach as he thought about the impending gathering of the Task Force. He wasn't looking forward to the meeting.

The next morning, Dusty arrived at the designated conference room a few minutes early and was greeted by Jim Mitchell. Jim had always been a big champion of the work concerning employee engagement. As the CFO, he was absolutely convinced by the research that high levels of engagement are directly linked to high levels of productivity. Though Dusty shared the same conviction with a little less passion, he highly respected Jim and his opinion. Jim had always supported Dusty. He had been a source of invaluable feedback at crucial times when Dusty needed objective counsel.

Dusty knew Jim to be insightful, straight shooting and fair. In short, he trusted his leadership. Dusty had heard Jim say on numerous occasions, "Where trust is high, resistance is low. Therefore, change and progress come quickly. Conversely, where trust is low, resistance is high. Therefore, change and progress come slowly." Through Jim's influence, Dusty had grown to understand the importance of building high trust relationships.

"Good morning, Dusty," Jim said with a smile. "Thanks for agreeing to be a part of the Task Force again this time around. I am looking forward to getting your seasoned insights on how you think we can get some traction around engagement."

The word traction caused Dusty to have a brief flashback to

Where trust is high, resistance is low. Therefore, change and progress come quickly. Conversely, where trust is low, resistance is high. Therefore, change and progress come slowly.

his conversation with Fred Walters about the clutch.

"Happy to be invited," Dusty said reflexively, though it was a bit disingenuous.

Dusty wanted to ask Jim a few pointed questions that had been churning in his head, but before he could get the words out other team members began to fill the room. He decided to wait until he could catch Jim privately.

The meeting was basically what Dusty expected. It began with a review of the report, highlighting the "opportunities for improvement." Then, there was time spent comparing scores with those of other leading organizations in the industry. This, of course, was followed by some lively discussion about which areas potentially could provide a lift to sagging employee morale. It was déjà vu for Dusty. This ride was all too familiar. He wanted to get off of this emotional Ferris wheel, which was moving up and down and round and round but going nowhere. He knew exactly what was coming next – the assignment of going back to the various teams and conducting focus groups to garner additional feedback that could be thrown into the meat grinder. He was about to explode with an objection, without any thought given to offering a solution, when the meeting took an unexpected change of course.

Jim stood for the first time during the meeting. Up to that point, he had primarily listened. As a veteran facilitator, he was a master of asking catalytic questions. However, now it was time for him to speak. His face and tone conveyed his intensity. He had everyone's full and undivided attention.

"If our company was a car, I would say that we are long overdue for a tune-up or possibly an engine overhaul. If we want to run smoothly and efficiently, it's time to do a multi-point checkup. Given all that we have discussed today, there are a few questions that I want you to ponder. Since our efforts in the past have failed to achieve the desired results, how can we do things differently this time around? After all, it was Albert Einstein who said, 'Problems cannot be solved by the same level of thinking that created them.' We need to look at engagement through a whole new lens.

"We are going to meet again in a week. In the meantime, I want you to give this your highest level of thinking. I believe we have the collective intelligence to provide some clarity for our organization. I don't want you to look at what our competitors are doing. Excellence never comes by comparing yourself to others. If by comparison we think we are better than others, then pride sets in and we have a tendency to gloat. If we fall short in our comparison to others, then we may struggle with morale issues and a sense of inferiority, which can negatively impact performance. Instead, I want us to own our destiny and dream a dream that will inspire everyone to bring their best to the table each and every day. I want us to reach our full potential as individuals and as a company."

Jim projected a slide onto the screen that read:

A Compelling Culture is Created When People:

- **BELIEVE the best IN each other**

- **WANT the best FOR each other**

- **EXPECT the best FROM each other**

Then, he continued, "I want us to craft a culture where we believe the very best *in* our people, provide the very best *for* our people and call out the very best *from* our people. As leaders, we know exactly what we want *from* our people. But what do we want *for* our people? Do we have a culture of high trust that believes the best *in* our people while we seek the best *for* our people? What would that look like and what is it going to take to get us there? When we answer these questions, we will be moving in the right direction. How do we chart a course with such a heading?"

With Jim's questions wafting in the air, the meeting was adjourned. Dusty sat there shell-shocked and motionless for a moment. He had been presented with a challenge before he could utter his objection. Nonetheless, he liked it. The challenge actually gave him hope that things might be different this time around. He could hardly wait for the appointment to get his oil changed.

Chapter Four

The Oil Change

Dusty finally remembered late Wednesday night to tell his wife, Lisa, that he was going to get the oil changed in her car the following afternoon. In response, she reminded him that it had been changed recently and wasn't due for another thousand miles. Dusty was certain this was the only time in their entire marriage that she had actually remembered when the oil had been changed. Concealing his dismay, Dusty explained that he was really trying to get some personal time with Fred Walters to discuss a few business matters.

"Then, why didn't you just ask him to meet you for coffee instead of going to the added expense of changing the oil when it's not needed?" Lisa asked insightfully.

Dusty wondered why her memory was serving her so well all of a sudden. And, since when had she become so logical? These thoughts were echoing so loudly in his head, in fact, that Dusty was afraid Lisa might hear them. He quickly asked her a question to divert her attention.

"Would you care to drive the T-bird while I have your car?"

"No, I'm good. I know that's your baby. I have plenty of catching up to do around the house tomorrow," Lisa responded.

Good deal, Dusty mused. He was set for the day and he had refrained from saying anything that might not have served him well. He had done that before and spent more nights on the couch than he cared to count.

As he drove to the office the following morning, Dusty reflected upon the fact that his relationship with Lisa had certainly seen better days. Over the course of their nineteen-year marriage they had drifted apart. Their busy schedules and diverse personal interests had caused them to spend time in two separate social spheres, passing each other only long enough to exchange necessary information to fulfill their household responsibilities. Dusty had always defined himself by his work, spending an inordinate amount of time at the office. He was proud of the reputation he had garnered as a dedicated leader. For him, a strong work ethic meant being the first one in and the last one out of the office. On Saturdays, he justified his morning round of golf at the club as his reward for having worked so hard during the week. While golf with his buddies was personally refreshing, it left little time on the weekend for Lisa and their three children. Even when he was physically present, he was often emotionally absent.

Lisa, likewise, had replaced her longing for Dusty's attention and affection with a busy social calendar. She joined the tennis team at the country club. She volunteered at the local elementary school, and she had an assortment of activities in the community in which she had become actively involved. It seemed like the only time that they were together as a family was when they were in church on Sunday mornings. It was a commitment that both Dusty and Lisa felt was worthwhile, but one that had become more obligatory over time. They wanted their three children to be exposed to the positive moral messages. Each week, however, they found themselves listening to the sermons, silently hoping that the other would apply the principles taught rather than seeking to grow personally. Even while sitting side by side in the sanctuary, they felt like strangers.

They rarely spoke of anything significant, such as their hopes and dreams or personal needs. An absence of deep emotional connection and the lack of intimacy primed the pump for frequent conflict. When they weren't fighting, a constant tension filled the air. Resentment had taken root in their relationship, and daily exchanges were all too often filled with caustic comments and signs of contempt. They demonstrated very little patience toward one another and, worse still, there was a growing sense of emptiness that Dusty felt toward Lisa. Dusty wasn't happy in their relationship and he knew that Lisa wasn't either. They had been sucking the lifeblood out of each other like two leeches locked in a deadly depleting hold on one another. Frankly, he didn't know how much longer they could hold it together – or if he really wanted to anymore.

Pulling into the parking lot, he forced his thinking to shift to what was on his agenda for the day. He tried to push the cares and concerns about his relationship with Lisa into the closet of his mind, but he knew all too well that he couldn't completely separate his personal life from his professional life. Every time he engaged in these intense mental gymnastics it left him frustrated and inevitably it had a negative impact on his work. He could suppress his negative emotions only so long before they began to leak over into other personal interactions. Nonetheless, he put on his best game face, picked up his pace, and entered the office with a contrived cheery persona.

After packing a full day into fewer hours, he was out the door and heading to Classic Car Care. He arrived a few minutes before his scheduled appointment and walked into the main waiting area. Fred was seated in one of the leather chairs talking with a customer about vintage trucks. He introduced Dusty to his friend, a car collector who always brought them to Fred for maintenance. After a brief but cordial conversation, the gentleman excused himself and left Dusty and Fred to be about their business.

"I'm here to get the oil changed in Lisa's car," Dusty said.

"Oh, skip that," Fred retorted. "I checked the records. Unless you've taken several road trips in the last few weeks, I really don't think it's due for a change. Let's walk around the corner and get some coffee!"

"Well, okay," Dusty chuckled under his breath.

He tried to contain his laughter so that he wouldn't have to reveal the content of his recent conversation with Lisa. Once at the coffee shop, they both ordered an iced coffee and sat at a table on the patio. It was a beautiful spring afternoon. The cool drink was the perfect beverage to offer the right balance of refreshment and caffeine to kick-start the conversation. Fred opened the door.

"So, to what do I owe the honor of you seeking me out for an oil change that you really don't need?" Fred asked curiously.

Dusty was busted and a little embarrassed. "Well, I really wanted to continue our conversation about engagement, and I could use a little business advice."

"You want business advice from a mechanic?"

"I am sorry to say that I never connected the dots until the other day. You've probably forgotten more about running a business than I will ever know, and I really would like to pick your brain," Dusty said.

"Well, in spite of what Howard Levine says, I would like to think that I still have a few nuggets of wisdom left to be mined somewhere between my ears. I would be happy to offer advice where I think it might be helpful, but I won't attempt to bluff you if it's outside my value grade." Dusty had never heard that term before. He knew quite well what a pay grade was, but value grade? He asked Fred what he meant by that.

"Life," Fred said, "is all about creating value. The secret to fulfillment is in seeking to bring value to every endeavor. Pay grade speaks to the kind of value that you *extract from* the organization. Value grade speaks to the kind of value that you *create for* the organization. I'm not interested in posturing myself or seeking to leverage opportunities for personal gain. That may work for awhile, but sooner or later folks will figure out that you are all about *YOU*.

> **Life is all about creating value. The secret to fulfillment is in seeking to bring value to every endeavor.**

"On the other hand, if I am always looking to enrich the lives of others or bring added value to my work environment, then my contributions will become evident and my work will be rewarded for what it truly is – a valuable contribution. When your value grade exceeds your pay grade, then you become invaluable to the organization – if not indispensable. In this case, I promise to do my best to bring value in the area of my strengths, but I won't blow smoke your way if it's beyond my personal knowledge and experience."

As Dusty was wrapping his head around that concept, Fred shifted gears. "Now, let's get right to business. Let's talk about your oil change."

The Oil Change

"But, I thought you said that the car didn't need an oil change?"

"It doesn't. I'm not talking about Lisa's car. I'm talking about either you or your business, or both. I assume you want something to change or you wouldn't have sought me out for advice. Is that correct?"

"Well, yes. But you don't even know what the issues are yet." Dusty said a bit perplexed.

"I don't have to know the issues to know that you are seeking a change and in order for change to lead to growth, there must always be an injection of something fresh to keep the parts moving properly without binding," said Fred. "You want something to shift and you need fresh 'oil' to make that happen. So, before we talk about the issues, let's talk first about change.

"Change is inevitable and it always begins with a situation – a clutch situation," Fred said as he took a pen from his freshly pressed shirt pocket and started to write on a napkin.

"Each clutch situation will either lead to personal growth or it will produce pain. At this pivotal point, we have a choice to make. If we embrace the situation and engage in the change process, we have the opportunity for personal growth.

"If, on the other hand, we become defensive and resistant to change, then we forfeit an opportunity for growth and just see the situation as a hardship. And typically hardships are seen as situations to be endured. Whether you see the clutch situation as a hardship or an opportunity for growth all depends upon your perspective. It's a matter of choice. We all have been given the wonderful privilege and opportunity to choose. It is both a personal right and a responsibility. It's what I like to call the *Either / Or* Factor. *Either* we choose to resist change and stagnate …*Or*, we choose to embrace the situation and grow. Choosing to grow leads to transformation, while choosing otherwise leads to degeneration. You see, we all get to make our own choices freely in life, up to a certain point – and then, our choices begin to make us! Ultimately, we all become the product of our choices."

We all get to make our own choices freely in life, up to a certain point – and then, our choices begin to make us!

"What exactly do you mean?" Dusty asked.

"Take the situation with Lisa's car. You didn't need an oil change yet, but let's say that you did. You know you need to change the oil, but you never make the choice and take the action necessary to change it. You could, but you justify your lack of action. You may claim that you are too busy. You rationalize that it will be all right to go a little longer without changing the oil. It is an inconvenience to slow down from your other obligations to address it. You have multiple opportunities, but you still don't make the right choice to change it. You resist or procrastinate in doing what you know is necessary. Sooner or later that choice will catch up with you. After a while, you may throw a rod and then the engine freezes up. Now, the choice not to change your oil has begun to shape your future. It has left you with another choice – a more expensive choice. Now you have to choose to replace the engine or buy another vehicle – a choice you were forced to make because of a series of poor choices. Sure, the right choice may have cost you a little time and money initially, but it would have kept you on the road. I see people all the time in life and in business making choices that limit their futures. Poor choices narrow your options, while good choices open a whole new vista of opportunities. Let me show you how that works."

Fred sketched on the napkin as he continued to talk.

"Let's talk about the upward spiral of growth, or what I like to call 'shifting into growth gear.' When a clutch situation arises and we choose to embrace it, that situation becomes an opportunity to seek and apply new truth. And truth applied leads to transformation. The 'oil' that makes shifting into growth gear possible without grinding is humility. Humility allows us to see ourselves honestly, without pretense, and leads to greater self-awareness. Humility is an acknowledgment of our humanity. It is the awareness that we are not perfect and we have no need to posture ourselves as being perfect. The fact is that we all have room for growth. Unfortunately, many people are stunted in their growth because they are self-deluded, believing things about themselves that simply are not true. Rather than embracing the challenge of change, they resist and try to posture themselves in a flattering light. But without honesty and humility, valucentricity is virtually impossible."

Humility is the 'oil' that allows you to shift smoothly into growth gear.

Dusty had no idea what Fred meant by "valucentricity," but he didn't want to interrupt Fred's train of thought, so he let him continue.

"Self-awareness comes through honest introspection and evaluation. A healthy evaluation of a situation causes us to see ourselves as we truly are and weigh the options and potential outcomes of our actions. It forces us to stop and consider the factors involved and extrapolate our choices to logical conclusions. Candid evaluation launches us on a journey to seek truth. However, the extent to which we find truth is directly proportionate to our openness and willingness to receive it. There is a proverbial saying that goes like this: 'When the student is ready, the teacher will appear.' Dusty, the answers to your questions are within your reach. They always have been. But you have to ask the questions before you can receive the answers. Now, you are finally beginning to ask."

Dusty thought Fred was beginning to sound more like a Buddhist monk than a business advisor. But, he suspended his judgment a little longer and asked Fred to continue.

"Once you ask, you open yourself up to receiving answers. The funny thing is that so many people never ask profound questions. Maybe they feel that asking is a sign of weakness. They may choose to pretend to have all the answers themselves. It could be that in not asking, they may feel more self-sufficient. Whatever the reason, it is almost always driven by pride. And pride always appears before a fall."

"So, ask and you shall receive," Dusty quipped, with an obvious edge of skepticism and sarcasm in his tone.

"In a way, yes!" Fred responded. "You see, Dusty, you are always going to receive something from somebody. The question becomes, 'Receive what from whom?' There will always be an abundance of folks who are willing to offer their opinions. What you have to determine is to whom will you listen and what will you receive? A good student learns best by asking the right questions and then selecting wisely whom he will allow to provide him with the answers. It is really pretty simple. You must choose carefully whom you will allow to influence your decisions. Good counsel perpetuates good choices. Bad counsel perpetuates bad choices. Good counsel amplifies valucentricity and bad counsel short circuits valucentricity."

There was that term again. Dusty wanted to delve into what

it meant but he was a bit embarrassed about his last comment, so he held his tongue a little longer.

Fred continued, "One of the keys to growth is asking great questions. If you ask poor questions, you are likely to get poor answers. If you ask good questions, you are likely to get good answers. But if you ask profound questions, and are willing to listen with humility, then often you will get profound answers."

"I'm not sure that I understand what you mean. Would you tell me a little more about the three types of questions?" Dusty asked.

Poor questions produce poor answers. Good questions produce good answers. But, profound questions often will produce profound answers.

"Sure," Fred responded. "Let's say that something has gone wrong with a project at work. As you convene the team and bring the situation to the table, poor questions might be, 'Who is to blame for getting us into this dilemma?' and 'Why did it happen?' Poor questions usually revolve around problems and personalities. They frequently are attempts to shift blame or get people to side with us to see things from our perspective. They involve posturing. By asking poor questions, what we really are seeking to do is deflect responsibility or affirm our position and ourselves. The answers may make for lively conversation but they are never helpful. Even if we successfully assign blame, we are no closer to resolving the problem.

"Good questions, on the other hand, seek to understand exactly what took place. A good question might be something like, 'What went wrong and how can we prevent it from happening again?' Good questions guide us toward a better understanding of the factors at play but they stop short of getting us to any reasonable resolutions. However, profound questions get to the heart of the matter. They open new worlds of possibilities and hold hope for change because they dissect the dysfunction that led to the problem and they set up the solution. Great questions focus on the fix. A profound question would be, 'What can we learn from this and how can we leverage that knowledge to solve the problem?' When you move beyond personalities and problems and shift the thinking to a solution-oriented perspective, it becomes inspirational. When you get to the solution side, people are much more likely to roll up their sleeves and get to work.

"In short, growth itself is inspirational. When people are authentic and are open to change, then others are drawn into the process and are inspired to be open and honest as well. If there is defensiveness and resistance, people pull away from each other for self-protection and emotional barriers are erected. When authenticity and humility are present, unity is often the result. And unity is the most powerful force in the universe for the creation of good. Unity enhances value creation. And it all begins by being honest with yourself about who you are. Humility is the 'oil' that allows you to shift smoothly into growth gear."

As he had been talking, Fred had written three key thoughts across the bands which spiraled up from the clutch situation. Dusty paused to look at each of them and pondered their significance in light of their conversation.

"So," Dusty interjected for the sake of clarification, "in each clutch situation we have a choice to make. We can either adopt an attitude of humility and embrace change or we can become defensive and resist change. Humility allows us to evaluate the situation and ourselves honestly and shifts us into growth gear. Growth always has a solution orientation. And growth creates unity and inspiration. I get all of that. But what do you mean by valucentricity?"

"I was wondering how long it was going to take you to ask me about that. Let me make a quick run to the restroom and when I get back we can talk about what valucentricity means," Fred responded.

Dusty was leaning into the conversation so much that he almost slipped off the edge of his chair when Fred stood up. He excused himself and went inside, leaving Dusty to wrestle with his thoughts for a few minutes. The hook was certainly set. Dusty was obviously on the line. Dusty examined the drawing on the napkin until Fred returned.

SHIFTING INTO GROWTH GEAR

- UNITY / INSPIRATION
- SOLUTION - ORIENTATION
- HONEST EVALUATION

CLUTCH SITUATION

Pay grade speaks to the kind of value that you extract from the organization. Value grade speaks to the kind of value that you create for the organization. When your value grade exceeds your pay grade, then you become invaluable to the organization – if not indispensable.

SECTION TWO

ALIGNMENT

Chapter Five

Valucentricity

After a few minutes, Fred returned to the table. He was now ready to reel Dusty into a whole new way of seeing his situation.

"Value-centric," Fred re-engaged, "simply means that values are at the very core of who you are and what you do. Your values determine how you see the world and respond to it. Or, you could say that a person's world-view is shaped by values. Valucentricity, then, is the energy and momentum that can be produced when values are properly aligned. It is like the spark that ignites the gas to create internal combustion. Or, think electricity. Electricity is a type of energy found in nature, but it can be man-made as well. Likewise, there is a natural structure of value in the universe. When we intentionally choose to align values, those values create a circuit through which power can flow. When we understand value alignment and value creation, we can craft movements of good through which positive energy can flow to light up the world."

Valucentricity is the energy and momentum that can be produced when values are properly aligned.

"I think I am following you, but please continue," Dusty prompted.

"Well, each person sees the world through a unique lens, which is crafted by the prioritization of certain values. Have you ever wondered how two people can experience the same situation and come away from it with two totally different interpretations of the event? You see, we can actually choose to 'spin' reality any way we want, depending upon what we choose to emphasize. That is what I call subjective reality. Think of the politician whose positions constantly morph to match the changing winds of the polls. He is choosing to create his own reality. Or, more accurately stated, he is letting the opinions of others shape his own reality. That subjective reality cannot last for long. Sooner or later objective reality - that which is inescapable and cannot be spun - will show up. And, when it does, a person's character is revealed through his values. Such a person might value power or popularity more highly than integrity. Whatever the case, his values are distorted and will sooner or later expose his judgment. Or, as some in the South are fond of saying: 'Whatever is down in your well will eventually come up in your bucket!'

"The more closely my subjective reality aligns with objective reality, the healthier, happier and more resilient I will be. In organizational life, if my values align with those of others, then greater synergy and positive energy will be the result. There is great power in identifying, clarifying and aligning values. That power is valucentricity.

"You see, a person's values are the most accurate predictor of what will come up in his bucket. There is actually a science dedicated to understanding how values shape a person's perspective on life and work. That science is called axiology. Axiology is the study of values and value formation and how they impact our thought processes, decision-making and performance. The father of modern axiology, Dr. Robert S. Hartman, postulated that all of our choices are value-driven. According to him, values form the foundation for all human behavior. Hartman dedicated his life to defining and studying the concept of *'good.'* For him, something was good if it *possessed all the properties necessary to fulfill its purpose.* Good, in Hartman's thinking, is all about fulfilling one's personal potential. It has more to do with pursuing excellence than it does with success. Success is often measured in comparison to what others have done, which is always a self-defeating proposition.

You will inevitably come up on the short end of the stick when compared to enough others.

Good, however, is about the pursuit of excellence – comparing yourself to your capabilities and seeking to become all you were meant to be. Good, then, is defined as functioning fully and effectively to maximize your strengths, passions and capabilities. As such, the creation of good could be considered humanity's most lofty pursuit. Hartman was consumed with the idea that good could actually be measured and that movements of good could be created by applying certain principles."

> **Good, then, is defined as functioning fully and effectively to maximize your strengths, passions and capabilities. As such, the creation of good could be considered humanity's most lofty pursuit.**

Dusty had never heard of axiology. But what Fred was saying about behavior being driven by values certainly made sense. Dusty wondered how he could have completed his post graduate studies and never heard of such a science. He took out his phone and drafted a memo so that he would remember to look up axiology and Robert Hartman.

Then, he asked Fred, "So, how did you become familiar with the principles of axiology?"

"Ah … for that, I forever will be indebted to my good friend and former roommate, Howie. At his insistence, we rented an apartment in New Haven, Connecticut, and enrolled in a summer course under Dr. Hartman when he was a visiting professor at Yale. We were not disappointed. We both became enamored with his teachings and the principles of axiology that could be applied to craft a more compelling corporate culture."

That was all that Dusty needed to hear. Fred's testimonial was convincing in and of itself, but the fact that Howard Levine had used the same principles solidified Dusty's resolve to learn as much as he could about axiology.

"So valucentricity is power produced through alignment of strong morals?" asked Dusty.

"A person's morals are definitely a part of the equation," Fred responded, "but there is more to it than that. Your moral values will certainly find expression in your daily decisions. But let me see if I can explain it more clearly. It may make more sense to say that valucentricity refers to the energy that can be created when you place the proper emphasis on certain aspects of life. It is about alignment of one's perspective and priorities. When we speak of values, we often think of ethical values – those deeply held personal convictions that typically have a spiritual foundation. We may think of ethical values in terms of what is right, moral and just. But there are also values that are more functional in nature.

These values represent tradeoffs that people make based upon what is deemed to be more important or holds higher value for that individual. These values impact how a person views himself, his world and how he relates to others. So, it can be said that, 'How we *view* things will drive how we *do* things.'

How we view things will drive how we do things.

"Another way of expressing it is to say that a person's values are the results of how he valuates – or prioritizes – certain aspects of life and work. By assessing the value that someone places on different elements, we gain insight and understanding as to how that individual is likely to function. Understanding one's values provides a framework for effective human interaction. It also forms the foundation of an individual's judgment capacity. So, as I said earlier, the more our personal values align with the natural structure of value in the universe, the healthier and more productive we will be as human beings. Thus, alignment generates valucentricity."

"Now you are really starting to sound like a spiritual advisor," Dusty interjected.

"Ah, maybe so, Grasshopper!" Fred whispered with a smile. "There certainly is a spiritual component to valucentricity. Most religions known to man are grounded on the ideals of treating others with honor, dignity and respect while doing everything within one's power to fulfill his or her God-given potential. At the same time, clarity and proper alignment of values provides the foundation for someone to live on purpose."

"Live on purpose?" Dusty sputtered inquisitively.

"Yes," Fred responded, "living on purpose. Living on purpose means you live purposefully, with purpose, and for a purpose. *For a purpose* defines the *what*. It answers the question, 'To what end?' To be remarkable, this *'what'* must be larger than self, providing a focus that is outward in nature and creates value for others. *With purpose* is about the *how*. It speaks to the passion, enthusiasm and creativity that one brings to the effort. It is the intensity *with* which a person pursues the *what*. And, purposefully implies both inspiration and intentionality. It is the *why*. It provides the motivation, because the *why* brings meaning and significance to any endeavor. At its core, purpose defines the *what*, the *how*, and the *why* of remarkable activity. And, I might add, purpose is always value-based, because it is the deepest expression of that which one holds most dear. So, 'on purpose' means that one is purposeful in the approach, passionate and undeterred about a purpose, and focused on a purpose beyond self.

"Living on purpose involves assuming personal responsibility for your own thoughts, feelings and actions. So many people simply drift through life being swept away by circumstances. Living on purpose is living with intentionality. It's life by design, not by default. It's about thinking for yourself and learning how to live above your circumstances. Rather than being negatively influenced by your environment, you are determined to influence your environment in positive ways. This sense of ownership adds clarity and quality to your decision-making processes. When you are living on purpose, you fully own your choices and take responsibility for your actions. Simply stated, you no longer fall prey to 'The Other Guy Syndrome' – that tendency to blame others for your circumstances," said Fred.

Dusty chimed in, "I know exactly what you mean about 'The Other Guy Syndrome.' I have a friend who is a defense attorney. He says that all of the people in prison are innocent according to their own testimony. He laughs when he says that everyone currently incarcerated would be released if we just could catch 'The Other Guy!'"

"Exactly," Fred chuckled as he continued. "But when you are living on purpose, you don't blame other people for your actions, nor do you excuse them because of the circumstances. You exert the power and the will to live out your values consistently. And, when your values are clearly defined and aligned, you live out of the core of your convictions. You are no longer dependent upon the actions of others to guide you and make you happy. Nor is your emotional well-being dependent upon the environmental conditions that surround you. Confidence and peace begin to mark your life as you take control of your inner world.

"Stress, on the other hand, is created when we are not living out our values consistently. Stress is ever-present, but it is worsened when our actions do not align with our beliefs. It creates what psychologists call cognitive dissonance – meaning that it creates turmoil in the mind and heart and robs a person of a sense of peace and harmony. But that's enough for now. We've been treading in deep water long enough for our first swimming lesson.

"My, how time flies when you are preaching on a soapbox," Fred quipped. "Let's pick up the conversation here next time. That is, if you are interested in exploring the topic a little further."

"You would be willing to meet again?"

"Sure, as long as you don't try to schedule another unnecessary oil change," Fred chided.

"Could you carve out an hour next Thursday?" Dusty asked, seizing upon the offer.

"Same time next week – you got it," Fred said, sporting his Cheshire cat grin.

On purpose means you live purposefully, with a purpose, and for a purpose.

✺

Chapter Six

On Purpose

When the Engagement Task Force convened again on Tuesday morning, Dusty was ready. He had done his homework. His head was racing with thoughts and ideas, but he knew he would have to edit himself before speaking. He felt as if he had been drinking water from a fire hose the past few days while doing his research, and he knew his colleagues wouldn't respond well if he spewed all over them. He was fully aware he would have to introduce some of his ideas slowly, so it would not to ruffle the feathers of those who had developed deep emotional attachments to the work that had been done previously.

Jim opened the meeting with a few words of introduction to tee up the discussion: "When we last met, I asked you to apply your best thinking to this issue of engagement. As I said the last time we were together, we need to figure out who and what we want to become, and then take the necessary measures to inspire the best in our people! Growth is necessary for us to fulfill our potential. How are we going to do that?" he asked. "The floor is open for your observations and suggestions. I'm counting on this conversation to spark our imaginations. Let's do some creative brainstorming and some good work today."

Jim's words reverberated in Dusty's head. His mind began to make word associations. When Jim said "*grow*," Dusty immediately thought *getting into growth gear*. When Jim said "*good*," Dusty thought *fulfilling one's personal potential – pursuing excellence*. He was beginning to scare himself with how quickly thoughts were coming to his mind, so he decided to sit there and scribble a few notes while others spoke first. The conversation followed the familiar course. There was talk about those areas in which the survey revealed low scores. Then there was the usual banter about which issues, if addressed effectively, could help to gain the greatest lift. This was followed by an emotional conversation about what had and had not worked in the past. Lines were being drawn and defenses were being built. Dusty started to feel like he was on a merry-go-round that was spinning too fast. He was becoming nauseated. His body language must have given him away because Jim brought him directly into the middle of the fray with a question.

"Dusty, you've been unusually quiet. What thoughts do you have to offer about all of this?"

Dusty took a deep breath and swallowed. He wasn't uncomfortable speaking his mind. Quite the contrary – he wanted to measure his words so that they would have the most impact.

"My thoughts run along two lines, Jim. First, when it comes to engagement, I wonder if we are measuring the right things. A lot of the questions on our survey are designed to determine how satisfied folks are with certain environmental factors. I, for one, am not sure that is an accurate reflection of engagement. A stronger indicator of engagement may be a healthy assessment of our culture. Culture is the collective expression of the values, thoughts and behaviors that individuals bring to the organization. Culture is *who you are* as a company – not *what you have* or even *what you do*. If the culture is healthy, then high engagement is almost certain. Engagement is simply a symptom of the cultural condition of the organization.

"Engagement is often defined as the emotional attachment that people feel toward an organization or endeavor. I have come to believe that a person's emotional attachment to their work will be determined by whether or not their personal values align with organizational values. There is great power in the alignment of values, or what one might call valucentricity. Valucentricity creates synergy, by which movements of good can be created.

"Secondly, if we are really trying to '*engage, empower and enrich*' the lives of our associates, maybe we need to begin to think in terms of doing less for them and equipping them to do more for themselves. What if instead of being influenced negatively by less than stellar environmental conditions, our people began to assume responsibility for making a positive impact on their environments. Rather than passively conforming to the surroundings, they could become agents of change. If we encourage them to take more initiative in creating value, how might it impact the work environment? If we could empower our people by teaching them to live on purpose – which is simply living intentionally and assuming personal responsibility for their own thoughts, feelings and actions – I think it could be revolutionary."

"All right, you have our attention," Jim said, "but can you unpack those ideas a little more and help us wrap our minds around them?"

"Well, think of your favorite philanthropic organization. It probably has a significant number of volunteers involved in the work. Those volunteers give their time, energy and resources freely to the work of the organization. Many of those folks make significant sacrifices simply for the sake of the cause. In corporate ranks, we use money as a primary motivator. But, in a volunteer organization, compensation is not even a factor. That kind of passionate commitment and discretionary effort is the result of an alignment of values. They believe deeply in a mission and they are called to align with a cause. I think there is much we could learn from studying volunteer organizations. If we understood how values influence human behavior and the power that can be harnessed by identifying and properly aligning values, it could be truly transformational.

"I wonder how many other environmental factors have little to do with tapping into the passion of our people. Rather than coming up with costly corporate initiatives, what if we helped team members more clearly define and live out their values? What if we could empower them to think about life and work differently? What if we could teach our associates how to make decisions out of conviction rather than convenience? And, what if we tapped into their strengths and passion to energize their work every day? What could happen if each team member became a change agent for good?"

Dusty was on a roll. He was beginning to feel like an impassioned preacher. The only problem was that he had exhausted the content of his sermon. There was a pause. Then, the inevitable question came...

"How do you suggest that we do that?"

There was a lengthy awkward silence. While he flipped through his notes, Dusty frantically scrolled through his freshly constructed mental Rolodex of information he had gleaned from Fred and his research. No answers were readily available. Finally, Jim came to his rescue.

"I think we may be onto something here. I am anxious to hear how you might suggest we put legs to some of these concepts. I have to tell you that I am intrigued with the ideas of valucentricity and living on purpose. If I understand what you are saying, then purposeful living could be described as living out your values in a mature and meaningful way. I like that. In relating to some of our team members, I am bothered by an immaturity that is reflected in what I would describe as an attitude of entitlement. There seems to be a general expectation of getting more in exchange for doing less. This has to change if we are going to survive. And, we have always placed a heavy emphasis on our corporate values. Dusty, I want to hear your thoughts about how all of this might be played out in our corporate context. Can you come back to next Tuesday's meeting with a formal presentation of what you might envision for us moving forward?"

Now I've done it, Dusty thought. He had opened Pandora's Box. However, he was not one to challenge the status quo without offering suggestions for improvement. Besides, he thought, although Pandora released all manner of evil into the world, at least she retained the angel of Hope. Dusty was strangely hopeful that maybe this time around they could move the compass needle northward. So, he agreed to bring his thoughts to the table. Then, as quickly as he voiced his commitment, he began to panic. The thought that he would see Fred again in two days helped keep the attack at bay. By the time Thursday afternoon rolled around, Dusty was armed and ready to corner Fred with his questions.

✦

Chapter Seven

Creativity

Fred came moseying into the coffee shop at four o'clock in his usual khakis and pressed shirt with the Classic Car Care logo emblazoned on the pocket. Dusty had arrived early. He had one hour of Fred's time and he was going to maximize it. He had ordered them both drinks and was waiting at the table with his notebook open and his pen poised. Before Fred could sit down, Dusty fired his first question: "So how do you teach someone to live on purpose?"

"Good afternoon to you, too, Dusty," Fred chuckled. "I see that you are ready to receive some answers."

"I'm sorry," Dusty responded. "It's just that I am eager to understand how this might all apply to my situation at work. I had the opportunity to do some homework and I have come to believe that some of the principles found in axiology might just be the ticket to help us significantly improve our corporate culture. As I have come to understand it, you could say that a person's values explain how that person views and responds to his world."

"Sounds like you *have* done your homework!" Fred replied. "So let's get to your question. As we said last time, living on purpose is about choosing to live above your circumstances. In order to do that, you have to understand the maxims that guide value creation."

The Maxim of Creativity

"First," said Fred, "we have to talk about the Maxim of Creativity. Maxim is a word that is not commonly used, but it has wonderful implications. A maxim is a general truth, a principle or rule of conduct. Think of maxims as the best means to *maximize* your performance. And this first maxim is foundational. The Maxim of Creativity is about value creation. It states that as human beings, **we are designed to create value in life.** There are essentially two approaches to life: one seeks to *extract value from* every endeavor, and the other seeks to *create and bring value to* every endeavor. Some might say you have 'Givers' and 'Takers.' But, it is not quite that simple.

"You see, healthy people want to grow. Healthy people, by nature, want to improve and establish a sense of self-mastery. This emphasis on personal responsibility is the antithesis of entitlement. As people and organizations mature, so does a desire to make a positive contribution to the world and those immediately around us. We want our presence to make a positive difference. We want to be appreciated and affirmed for our work and the fact that we are able to bring something of value to the table in a way that only we can. Nobody wants to be disrespected, discarded or pushed aside as having no value or offering little of true value. We all want to leave a lasting legacy. This desire to bring value, however, can often be twisted into a drive to achieve. Some people think that life is defined and measured by pay scale and material possessions. It's the same mentality that says, 'He who dies with the most toys wins.' For some people, success is all about titles and trinkets. This is a perversion of a natural longing for significance that comes through value creation.

"A sense of satisfaction and significance comes from understanding who you are and how you can best bring value to every relationship and every endeavor in life. This is where the 'self-esteem movement' jumped the tracks and seriously derailed many young lives. Those who are big self-esteem proponents mistakenly try to protect the tender self-concepts of our young people. They don't want kids to feel inadequate because of comparisons, so competition is removed from our sporting programs. After all, to have a *winner* necessitates that you have a *loser* and nobody should be referred to as the *loser* – at least according to this line of thinking. Therefore, no scores are kept in younger athletic leagues. But, don't be fooled; the kids always know who wins the game! Likewise, everyone receives the same trophy or ribbon, no matter how well or how poorly they play. In other words, everyone is rewarded for nothing more than showing up. Consequently, we now have too many young people emerging in the marketplace who want to be rewarded just for showing up! And we call this attitude, *entitlement*. But, it's not altogether their fault. We set them up for it."

The Maxim of Creativity
We are designed to create value in life.
There are essentially two approaches to life: one seeks to ***extract value from*** every endeavor and the other seeks to ***create and bring value to*** every endeavor.

"I see where you are going with this," Dusty interjected. "Not that we teach our kids that you have to win at any cost, but in life the fact is that we are rewarded according to our performance and contribution. It is important to teach our kids to win with grace and lose with dignity. Either way they have to learn how to deal effectively with their emotions and responses. More importantly, a sense of responsibility encourages them to take whatever steps are necessary to improve rather than expecting others to run to their rescue or reward them for poor performance."

"Precisely!" Fred affirmed. "Everybody experiences loss in life. It is how you deal with it that really counts. You don't have to be defined by your losses. The people I know who possess the greatest character are those who have overcome their losses and challenges to rise victoriously on the other side. What we really need to teach our kids is that a healthy self-esteem comes from a healthy sense of self-worth. And self-worth comes from the conviction that you are a person of great value and the confidence of knowing that you've made a significant contribution to a good cause. In other words, self-worth comes from knowing you have created value."

Self-worth comes from the conviction that you are a person of great value and the confidence of knowing that you've made a significant contribution to a good cause. In other words, self-worth comes from knowing you have created value.

So, let me make sure that I have this right," Dusty interjected. "Your value grade, as you referred to it, is really a measurement of how much added value you bring to the table as a member of any team. It's a separate concept from that of a pay grade. There are people who may be high on the pay grade scale who actually bring very little added value to the organization. And conversely, there are others who are bringing value well beyond their pay grade. I would assume that ideally those who bring the greatest value to an organization should be compensated and rewarded for their contributions in order to share in the value that they have created. That value creation could come in the form of revenue generation or it could come from stellar service or the sharing of best practices. It might even be the value brought by those who have contributed the most in terms of collaboration or innovation."

"Yes," responded Fred, "but let me take it a step further. What we are looking for is valucentricity. Let's say that your top sales producer is also a pain in the posterior for everyone – a real prima donna. He may generate revenue, but his attitude may be cancerous. His presence may be *extracting as much value from* the team as he is *creating and bringing value to* the team through his sales efforts. The money he makes can never take priority over the way he treats people. Strong organizations always put people ahead of profits because they know that if you do right by your people – internally and externally – then the profits will follow. Therefore, the person who provides the greatest valucentricity is the person who brings both productivity and positive energy to the environment. In every situation we have a choice to make – we can either seek to *create value* or seek to *extract value*. Fulfillment comes through creating as much value as possible. Does that make sense?"

"It certainly does and it gives me a whole new way of evaluating each situation. It makes me think of all the metrics we use in the call center. Trust me when I say we know how to *do* metrics! We are a production-oriented, metrics-driven, spreadsheet-proliferating organization. But, the one thing we have not been able to accurately assess is the passion of our people. And we certainly haven't done anything to help our associates take full responsibility for their attitudes and contributions. Instead, we keep beating our heads against the wall trying to figure out what we can give our folks that will make them happier. Now, I realize that the best thing we can give them is an opportunity to utilize our mission and vision to create value through a worthy endeavor in which they can take pride and feel good about their contribution. If I understand what you are saying, energy levels will increase as people see that they are creating value for others and working toward a worthy cause."

"It sounds like you're getting it," Fred said with a grin. "Now, let me ask you a question."

"Fire away."

"How do most organizations approach value engineering?" asked Fred.

Dusty thought for a moment and then offered the perfect textbook answer. "Value engineering is based upon function and cost analysis. It is an attempt to get a better product to market faster and cheaper than competitors."

"Alright, that's a spot on definition," Fred acknowledged. "Given those three adjectives – better, faster and cheaper – which one is emphasized most often?"

"In my experience, the focus is almost always on cheaper. Cutting costs is typically seen as the clearest path to increasing margin for the manufacturer and value for the customer."

"That is what I have witnessed most often as well," Fred affirmed. "However, that approach stifles valucentricity. It takes no genius to cut costs. In the absence of creative energy, the default position is always to eliminate expenses. But, valucentricity is generated by focusing upon creating such a remarkable product or service for the customer that you deliver an experience worth repeating. And remarkable experiences have more to do with personal attention than they do with price point.

"If your focus is purely on numbers then the question becomes, 'How low can we drive our costs before our customers will no longer tolerate the quality of our product or service?' On the other hand, if your focus is on crafting a memorable experience, then the question becomes, 'How can we create so much value that our products and services become remarkable?' Valucentricity emphasizes making a difference over making a dollar. That difference is found in making meaningful emotional connections with people. If you are successful in making those connections, then your customers will happily pay full price for your services because they perceive you as offering more value. Every organization creates transactions. But, great organizations create powerful relationships through the superior value they bring to the table.

"You see, relationships trump transactions every time. And when the value you provide exceeds all expectations, then people will talk about it. You become remarkable! Robert Stephens, the founder of Geek Squad was fond of saying, 'Advertising is the tax you pay for being unremarkable.'"

"Wow, that's really good," Dusty affirmed. "Word of mouth is always the most powerful way for your message to be broadcast. And, I see now that it's the relationship that makes the referral so powerful. At the same time, value engineering should be more value conscious than cost conscious. Because the moment you concentrate on price, you've lost your creative energy. Focusing on numbers unplugs you from the power of valucentricity. Numbers will not produce value. Value produces numbers."

"I could not have said it better myself," Fred beamed. "Now, let's talk about the Maxim of Positivity."

Chapter Eight

Positivity

"As you just said, a person's energy level increases as the individual creates value. The Maxim of Positivity explains just how that happens. It states that, **_authentic positivity is the by-product of creating true value._** By positivity I am not referring to a Pollyanna attitude toward life or what some might describe as self-help hype and fluff. On the contrary, as we create true value for others, positive energy and emotion are natural byproducts of our actions. Positivity and valucentricity are synonymous. And value creation answers the question, 'How does someone experience the good in life?'"

Fred leaned in and asked a second question, "Have you ever noticed how happiness is so elusive? Literally, the harder you pursue it, the more frustrated you can become. Sir John Templeton said, 'Happiness pursued eludes, happiness given returns.' The same could be said for success. Some of the most successful people often don't think that they are. That's why they can be seen chasing their own tails to exhaustion. It's almost comical. The more you seek to be fulfilled, the less you actually experience fulfillment. This is because in the pursuit of these 'good' dimensions of life, the accent is often placed on the wrong syllable. These 'good' aspects of life are not ends in themselves or goals to be attained, but rather byproducts of creating value.

> *"Happiness pursued eludes, happiness given returns."*
>
> Sir John Templeton

"From a corporate perspective, think about the issue of innovation. Innovation, and the ability to adapt to a changing marketplace, is absolutely essential to the survival of any organization. However, the more a company attempts to systematize efficiency in the pursuit of innovation, the less likely that organization will experience great measures of it. The more structure, policies and procedures an organization puts in place to pursue innovation and the more pressure that is applied to produce it, the less likely it will occur. This is because pressure drains emotional energy that could and should be applied to nurture creativity. When that energy is siphoned off by rigid dictates and demands, the gravitational forces of efficiency keep the imagination earthbound.

"Often, the applied practices of Scientific Management actually act to quell innovation. That is not to say that there aren't disciplines that must be utilized in the creative processes. Those disciplines usually involve slowing, observing and questioning, which all take time. Time that is necessary for reflection and meditation on the *'what ifs'* and *'why nots.'* The idea of taking time for reflection is actually counterintuitive and flies in the face of process efficiency. But the reality is that if you want to create an environment of innovation, you need to give people time to think and dream – while on the clock. Give them the opportunity and resources to work on a solution to a problem or come up with a service that is of interest to them – something they really want to work on in an area where they can create the greatest possible value. The stated objective of this discretionary time should always be to employ their passion and their strengths to bring as much value to the organization as they possibly can. Then, step back and watch innovation take place."

While Fred was talking, Dusty's mind wandered momentarily. He reflected upon all the corporate initiatives, floated down from on high, that had failed to gain any momentum. Then, he thought about a community service project that had been initiated and championed by a few folks in one of the call centers. They had successfully rallied both the people and the resources to begin what was a modest local community project. In just two years, it had grown into an annual two-day event where associates from across the organization volunteered time in the community to work with local shelters and food banks. It was truly a grass roots movement that gained so much momentum that corporate embraced it. Literally everyone in the Atlanta offices had become involved.

"Success," Fred continued, "comes in much the same way. When I was in college, I thought the route to success was to get the highest GPA and build the best resume, in the hopes of getting the highest paying job. In doing so, I planned to position myself to extract as much value from my employment opportunities as possible. And it worked, for a season. I was hired by a mid-size technology firm and began to move up the corporate ranks. I was making good money, but honestly I wasn't enjoying myself. In order to assuage the internal conflict, I did what so many others do – I sold out to the next highest bidder. Someone was willing to pay me more money, so I switched teams. I became a mercenary in the marketplace. I wasn't any happier in the next role. But I justified the move by convincing myself that if I was going to be miserable doing what I was doing, at least I was going to make more money doing it. Of course, making more money didn't do anything to brighten my spirits or bring more enjoyment to my employment. The additional money never balanced the emotional scales for me. My entire focus was on extracting value rather than creating value.

"So many people enter the marketplace today with the same mentality. Success for them is all about getting a high-paying job. It has little to do with enjoying the work or whether or not their values align with the organization. It has less to do with passion and purpose than it does with the paycheck. Consequently, they see themselves as free-agents rather than long-term team members or employees. They sign on for a single season and then evaluate their position, based upon a variety of conditions that are all framed by value-extraction. You could call it a spirit of entitlement. Whatever you choose to call it, the decision has little to do with creating value and everything to do with 'what's in it for me?'"

Dusty began to squirm a bit in his chair, growing increasingly uncomfortable with the course of the conversation. Fred's recollection of his career so far sounded very similar to his own corporate journey. There had been many times in the past few years that Dusty had actually asked himself why he was doing what he was doing. He didn't interrupt Fred. Instead, he sat there hoping that the rest of the story would turn out to be a bit brighter.

"Then, Howie came along and everything changed for me. He offered me a partnership in a start-up company. I jumped at the opportunity to work with him. By that time, Howie was committed to applying the principles of value creation in day-to-day business. We began to craft our talent development initiatives and best practices around these very principles. We had a blast growing the company and its culture. And, I dare say we created an environment where people enjoyed working because they saw the value that they were bringing to the lives of our clients and, consequently, to the organization. Within twelve years, we had garnered a significant market share and the attention of our peers in the industry. When we were offered the opportunity to sell, we struggled with letting others come in and potentially change our model. As a part of the negotiations, we were both asked to stay on for a two-year transitional period to ensure that the culture would be perpetuated. We agreed. We continued to grow the company for those two years and then made our exit. Howie went on to his next gig and I made enough money to retire. It was exactly what I had wanted to do since I had planned my career path back in college. I was forty-one and retired! Being young and retired was incredible – for about six months.

"That's when I really experienced the full impact of value creation. As the first Maxim of Creativity states, we were designed to create value. I bored quickly of playing golf three times a week and going on solo fishing trips. It wasn't long before Anne started kicking me out of the house because I was getting on her nerves. Then, it dawned on me. I was miserable because I wasn't creating the kind of value that I knew I was capable of creating. So, I hoisted the flag and flew my colors again. Before I knew it, Performax, the company that had purchased us less than three years earlier, asked me to take over at the helm. It was a great run and I had the time of my life. When I finally did step down eight years ago, I opened up Classic Car Care. The fact is, I will never retire. Truett Cathy, the founder of Chick-fil-A, once said, 'If you love what you do, you will never work another day in your life.' I truly believe that. Now, I play with cars three days a week and get paid for it. The rest of my time is spent with Anne, the grandkids and serving on the boards of three philanthropic organizations. And, in each of these arenas, I seek to bring as much value to the table as I can.

> **"If you love what you do, you will never work another day in your life."**
>
> Truett Cathy, Founder of Chick-fil-A

"Like I said, I have discovered that success is a by-product of creating value. Happiness is a by-product of creating value. Significance is a by-product of creating value. Fulfillment is a by-product of creating value. I would even say that courage and optimism are by-products of creating value. We are designed to create value. You can create value organizationally and you can create value interpersonally. Creating value in relationships engenders trust and openness. It breeds camaraderie among colleagues. It fosters goodwill. It heals hurts. It offers forgiveness and second chances. At the same time, it holds people accountable for bringing their very best to the table in every endeavor."

Dusty wondered how this all might apply to his relationship with his 17-year-old son, Mike. Because Mike was the eldest of Dusty and Lisa's three children, they had high expectations for him. In moments of honest reflection, Dusty would acknowledge that he had ridden Mike pretty hard to excel in just about everything from academics to sports and summer internships that he felt would look good on Mike's college applications. Mike was a junior in high school and had always done well, but he was beginning to show signs of rebellion. Dusty had started to sense that Mike was carrying resentment toward him. He frequently spoke disrespectfully to him and to Lisa. And when Dusty reacted with heavy-handed disciplinary measures it only made matters worse. Mike would either lash out in return or withdraw from the family and shut Dusty out. He wondered what it might look like to create value in the relationship with his son. If there was one thing their relationship obviously needed it was positivity. Applying these principles to his closest relationships certainly deserved further reflection.

The Maxim of Positivity

Authentic positivity is the by-product of creating true value.

… uy6ut
SECTION THREE

ADJUSTMENT

Chapter Nine

Sustainability

"So, is that enough for today or do you want to continue?" Fred asked. "It's almost five o'clock and I want to be sensitive to your time."

"You certainly have my attention. I would like to continue if you don't mind. How many more maxims are there?"

"Two more! Let's discuss them and then we can call it a day."

"That sounds great to me," Dusty replied.

"The third is the Maxim of Sustainability. It says that in order **to continuously create value, leverage your passion and strengths to solve problems**. This principle is vital, but often misunderstood. So, let me break it down. There is a lot of white noise today about pursuing your passion. Motivational speakers are forever encouraging people to 'do what you love to do and the money will follow.' This is a misguided notion. I love to hit the little white ball, but I could never play golf for a living. Nobody would be foolish enough to pay me to play. I simply don't have the game. The reality is that if you do what you love and someone will pay you to do it, then great, you call that a job. On the other hand, if you do what you love and nobody will pay you to do it, it's nothing more than a hobby.

The Maxim of Sustainability
To continuously create value, leverage your passion and strengths to solve problems.

"Most people don't have the luxury of simply pursuing a passion. It is erroneous and dangerous to encourage people to limit their activity to 'doing what they love to do.' Few people can make a living that way. However, it is vital that people learn to 'love what they do.' For some, that may seem like a meaningless play on words, but I would suggest that it is far more than semantics. People must connect emotionally with their work in order for it to be meaningful. And making that connection falls largely on the shoulders of leadership. Good leaders inspire those around them to see the value in what they do. They work hard to ensure that personal values are aligned with corporate values. When they are, then emotional attachment to the work is the result. Inspirational leaders also connect the organizational objectives to personal passion. When people are emotionally engaged in their work, they are much more likely to offer discretionary effort. Loyalty, morale, and performance all increase when team members are highly engaged. People need to see that they are making a difference in the lives of others and contributing positively to the world. Sometimes that process begins by reframing someone's perspective of work."

"What do you mean when you say reframing their perspective?" Dusty asked.

"It is simply changing the way someone looks at the work experience. One of the most memorable quotes attributed to Howard Schultz, the CEO of Starbucks, goes like this: 'We're in the people business serving coffee, not the coffee business serving people.' This shift in emphasis changes the paradigm. It is not merely inspirational, it is revolutionary.

"Obviously, work should provide a product, service or solution. But, ultimately, it's about people and somehow making their lives better. When we see our lives as instrumental in creating value for others, then the work itself becomes much more meaningful."

> **"We're in the people business serving coffee, not the coffee business serving people."**
>
> *Howard Schultz, CEO of Starbucks*

"But, isn't that just a head game? I mean, after all, that's really nothing more than mental smoke and mirrors," Dusty said cynically.

"I'm not talking about denying or distorting reality. I am talking about redefining work so that the individual is inspired to see deeper value in what they are doing. Suppose I were to offer to pay you twelve dollars an hour to stand in a driving rain and fill large bags with sand. Would you be inspired by that offer?" asked Fred.

"Not really," Dusty responded nonchalantly.

"I didn't think so. But, let me see if your response changes if I reframe the question. Suppose I told you that your brother's home near the coast was being threatened by an oncoming tropical storm. The only way to stop the rising flood waters and save his home is to create a levee out of sand bags. He has called upon his friends and family to help. Now, would you be willing to fill sand bags in a driving rain?"

"Well, if you put it that way, of course I would. I would be willing to fill sand bags for days, if necessary, and there's no way I would take a dime," Dusty said passionately.

"That's what I suspected. Money could not motivate you enough to move you to action. However, the thought of helping your brother save his home inspired you to consider working tirelessly for a cause that aligned with what you highly value. The actual work didn't change. In fact, it was exactly the same. But your perception of the work dramatically changed. Your paradigm shifted. That is the power of reframing how one views work. You weren't inspired to trade your time for money. But, you were passionate and willing to work hard when you saw your efforts as being beneficial to someone that you cared about deeply. One of a leader's greatest responsibilities is to shift the emphasis of work from *'making a dollar'* to *'making a difference'* in the lives of others."

Dusty's eyes lit up.

"One of my favorite quotes is by Jim Collins, the author of *Good to Great*. He said, 'True greatness comes in direct proportion to passionate pursuit of a purpose beyond money.' Is that what you mean when you talk about living on purpose?" Dusty asked.

"Most definitely! You are living both on purpose and with purpose. You don't just have a mission – you are on a mission. Life becomes intentional and meaningful because you are in pursuit of a higher calling than merely monetary rewards. For profit companies do well when they operate with a philanthropic passion. Companies become remarkable when they are characterized by a deep desire to make the world a better place. In doing so, they create value for everyone. And making the world better taps into the passion of your people," Fred said as he drew a triangle on another napkin.

"Reframing one's situation to inspire passion is only one side of a triangle. With strong values serving as the base and passion on one side, the other side involves leveraging your individual strengths to create maximum value."

Fred began to write on each side of the triangle.

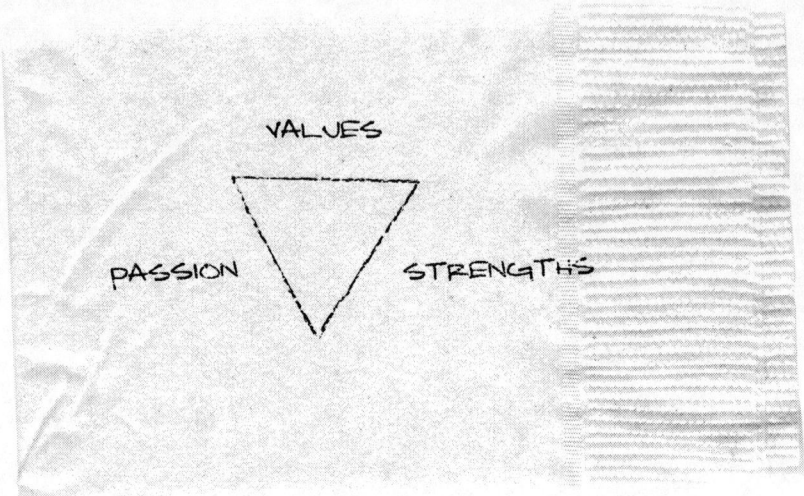

"Much has been written about discovering and applying a person's talents or strengths. The idea is that exponential results come, not by focusing on improving your weaknesses, but by leveraging your strengths. On this point, I could not agree more. Far too much time and energy is wasted in performance reviews on 'gap development'—the politically correct way of saying 'weaknesses.' Oh, we sometimes call them 'opportunities for improvement,' but the reality is that investing large amounts of time and energy here rarely pays rich dividends. Focusing on weaknesses keeps the spotlight on self. Focusing on strengths keeps the emphasis on how to bring value to others.

"I am not suggesting that people resist opportunities to stretch themselves in the development of new competencies. In areas that are outside of a person's strengths, certain minimal standards may need to be met to fulfill a given role or responsibility. If left unaddressed, an underdeveloped skill set could become an Achilles' heel that might cripple opportunities for advancement. Everyone can be encouraged to continually learn and grow to expand his or her knowledge and skills. What I am suggesting is that there are some things that you do naturally to near perfection with very little effort. Those are your strengths and they should be maximized. There are certain aspects of work that deplete your energy levels and other aspects that elevate your energy levels. For maximum productivity, you should seek to do more of the things that energize you and less of the things that drain you. When you are operating in your strengths, you might say that you are 'in the zone.' You experience maximum results with minimal effort. You are invigorated. Time flies and you feel confident and empowered when you are operating within your strengths."

Focusing on weaknesses keeps the spotlight on self. Focusing on strengths keeps the emphasis on how to bring value to others.

Dusty chimed in, "I am very familiar with the concept of strengths-based training. I think it's healthy to emphasize strengths rather than to harp on weaknesses. Trying to shore up weaknesses is like painting over rotten wood. It may look good for a season, but it won't have the strength to hold up the structure over time. Maximizing strengths is by far more productive. But how do you keep an emphasis on passion and strengths without pushing it to the edge of the slippery slope of entitlement?"

"Ah, that's a great question," Fred said with a smile. "Completing the maxim will address your concern. The most important element is found in the closing phrase. You have to apply passion and strengths ***to solve problems***. Here is where the rubber meets the road. Passion and strengths are superfluous if they are not applied to create value by producing effective solutions. Resolving a problem is about bringing something to the table that hasn't been a part of the equation before. Tackling tough issues allows us to effectively apply our passion and strengths. And value creation is directly proportionate to the size of the problem resolved. The bigger the problem may be, the greater the value in its resolution. The bigger the problem is, the greater the fulfillment and satisfaction that comes from solving it. The key is to look for the biggest problem you can find and take it on, applying your strengths and passion to fix it.

"Unfortunately, this is where so many people miss their greatest opportunities. What usually happens when a problem arises in the work setting? What do most folks do when they are challenged with a tough situation or a project gone awry?" queried Fred.

"They run the other way – if not physically, certainly

Sustainability

emotionally. They want to distance themselves from the problem and pass the responsibility for fixing it to someone else," Dusty answered. A tone of frustration marked his response.

"Correct. That is how most people react. But, the payoff is in creating the greatest value – valucentricity. And what better opportunity than when things are most challenging? If you are only interested in extracting value and preserving an image, then this is risky business. But if you truly want to make a difference, the next problem you encounter may very well be your chance. Look to give rather than to get. In a word – *Serve*. The more service you render, the more value you create. The more value you create, the more invaluable you become to the organization and to others." Fred once again took his pen and wrote beneath the point of the triangle.

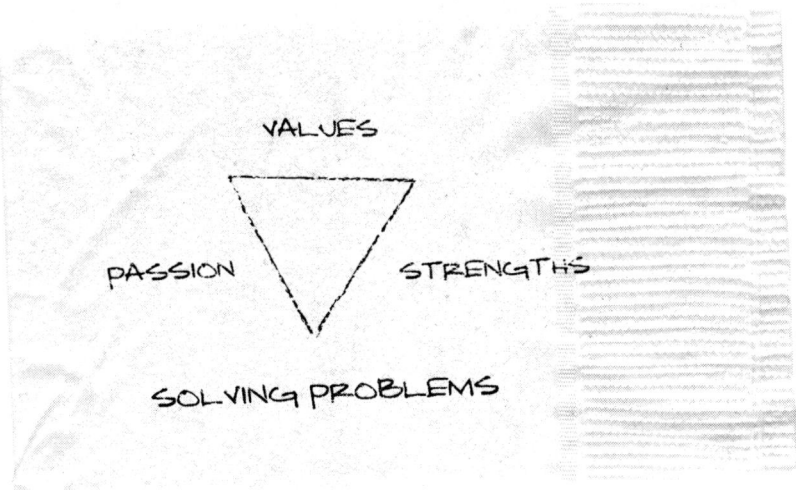

"I am familiar with the whole concept of Servant Leadership," Dusty interjected. "But, this really brings it into focus. What you are suggesting is that serving is about *creating value for* and not simply seeking to *extract value from* every relationship, encounter and endeavor. And the best way to sustain value creation is to engage people by making sure that their personal values align with corporate values. Then, you empower them to solve problems at the intersection of their passions and strengths. When you do that, you not only elevate productivity, but you also cultivate a culture of positivity. Do I have that all right?" asked Dusty.

"Yep!"

"So, how in the heck do you do that?" Dusty asked quizzically.

Chapter Ten

Choice

"Elementary, my dear Watson," Fred replied playfully. "You give them a choice."

"What do you mean?"

"A long time ago, a trusted mentor of mine gave me a bit of sage advice. He told me that, '*Nothing of long-lasting positive value ever happens by force.*' That is why domination and manipulation never work. You may be able to force your will upon others for a season, but it will ultimately fail. As soon as they get out from under your control, they will make their own choices. Everyone always does. And typically, the more coercion is applied, the less cooperation is experienced. It may look like cooperation on the surface, but it is usually nothing more than concession or compliance. Either way, there is little ownership or passion. I don't care if you are dealing with parenting issues, international political issues, an interpersonal issue with a colleague, or a corporate issue, people will always push back when they feel that someone is powering up on them. Ultimately, there will be a personal choice. It is the last great freedom."

Dusty's mind raced to a quote he had read in a book entitled, *Man's Search for Meaning*, written by Viktor Frankl. Jim Mitchell had encouraged Dusty to read the book as a part of a leadership development program at Query. Frankl was an Austrian neurologist and psychiatrist, as well as a Holocaust survivor. He spent years in a concentration camp and after having everything stripped away by his oppressors, he went on later to write: *"The last of the human freedoms – to choose one's attitude in any given set of circumstances, to choose one's own way."* That quote had been indelibly ingrained in Dusty's consciousness. He had always wondered how someone could endure such atrocities and still maintain any semblance of sanity, let alone civility. Now, he was beginning to understand – that, too, was a choice.

Nothing of long-lasting positive value ever happens by force.

"Do you remember when we talked about the fact that we all have been given the privilege and responsibility of choice?"

"Of course I do," Dusty said, opening his manila file folder and taking out the napkin on which Fred had scribbled the clutch situation and growth spiral.

"Well, as I said, every clutch situation presents a choice – an *Either / Or* choice. In each case you can seek to either *create value* or you can position yourself to *extract value*. As you probably remember, a clutch situation is any encounter that requires two or more parties to engage in order to make progress. To engage effectively, the interests of both parties must be taken into consideration. If you choose to *create value*, then you will naturally adopt a *We* mentality. You will seek to do what is best for all involved. A *Me* mentality, on the other hand, short-circuits any attempt to create valucentricity. So, in opting to *create value*, you are choosing to place *We* over *Me*. This allows you to evaluate the options and determine which one has the greatest potential for producing the best long-term outcomes for both parties. In other words, it sets you up to seek a win-win outcome in your efforts. It sounds like solid common sense to say that you should always put *We* over *Me*, but the reality is that the choice to *create value* is not always so easily made.

"Unfortunately, our natural tendency is to lean toward *extracting value* from most situations. By default, there is a bent within human nature to be self-centered and to do what's best for *Me*. Children don't have to be taught how to be selfish. They master that all by themselves. When asked to share with a friend or sibling, they can quickly and clearly express their rights of possession in a single word – Mine! They have to be taught through example how to share with others. As they grow older, the world reinforces that possessive attitude by teaching them to look out for number one and to ask in a thousand subtle ways, 'What's in it for me?' But the moment someone chooses to *extract value*, he automatically puts *I* over *Us*. And in doing so, an atmospheric condition is created that can range from mildly competitive to downright antagonistic. This choice to position one's self-interest over that of others and to *extract value* launches the individual into a downward spiral that ultimately leads toward alienation from others and desperation."

"I think I know where you are going with all of this, but play it out for me," Dusty said. "So, you are saying that seeking to *extract value* is in itself an act of selfishness. And in seeking to take care of me first and get what's mine puts me in a competitive place that might alienate me from others. But isn't competition a good thing? Doesn't it cause us to take our game to the next level? How could that be bad? Isn't capitalism itself driven by competitive markets?" Dusty asked, a bit perplexed.

"Competition is great when you are playing games. In games, the stakes are usually inconsequential. We play for the fun of the sport. But life isn't a game. You don't play life! If your winning means that someone else loses, then there can be devastating consequences relationally. It's not that competition itself is bad. Rather, it's the attitude and perspective that someone brings to the experience that makes all the difference. A perspective that says, 'I must win at all cost' is what I call a *Scarcity Mentality*. If I believe that there are only limited resources in the world and that in order to survive I must deprive someone else of those resources, then I will compete to *extract value* in each situation to ensure my survival. If, on the other hand, I possess an *Abundance Mentality*, then I come at life from a totally different vantage point. In that case, I believe that by *creating value* there can be an abundance of resources produced that may be shared by those who were involved in the creative process. Those who *create value* are rewarded. They are able to enjoy the value of what they have created through their efforts. And relationships are enriched in the process. All because an *Abundance Mentality* actually dictates that everyone handle resources responsibly for the greater good of all.

"Let me give you an example. My accountant, whom I've trusted for years, recently retired. He didn't listen very well when I explained value creation to him, so in about six months I expect he will become as bored as I did in my retirement. At that point, I am sure he will be primed for more meaningful conversations. In the meantime, however, I had to find another accountant to handle the books for Classic Car Care. We had several highly qualified people who were recommended to us. After making our selection, I sat down to 'negotiate' a deal with one particular CPA. After clarifying the responsibilities and expectations, I asked him what he would charge for his services. When he told me, I am sure that he expected me to counter by suggesting a lesser sum.

Instead, I think my response sent him into shock.

"I told him that I thought he was worth every penny and that we would be happy to pay him that amount for his services. You should have seen the look on his face. It must have been the first time anyone had ever said that to him. He sat there not knowing what to say. He was loaded and cocked with a comeback to the counter that never came. He expected me to negotiate with him on his fees. After a lengthy silence, he just smiled and shook my hand. Why do you think I did that?" Fred asked Dusty.

"I suppose because you really liked the guy," Dusty offered.

"Well, I do think he is superior in his skill sets, but that's not the reason. Suppose I had tried to contract his services for the least possible amount that I might have to pay. What if I had hammered him in a negotiation process? What kind of climate would that have established for our relationship moving forward?" Fred continued to query.

"It might have set him a bit on his heels, but you already said he was expecting you to negotiate his fees," Dusty responded.

"Exactly," said Fred. "So, how do you think he felt when I did the unexpected – offered to pay what he was asking for his services and told him that I wanted us to be 'trusted partners,' both committing ourselves to bring as much value to the table as possible for each other?"

"By his reaction, he was obviously surprised. He probably left feeling encouraged and committed to offering you his very best service. Chances are when others are competing for his time and attention, he will probably do everything within his power to make sure that you are taken care of first," Dusty offered.

"I have every confidence that he will do just that! On the other hand, if I had tried to beat him down on his fees, he likely may look for ways to hedge or cut services. He may even resent not making as much money as he could be working with other clients."

Then, Fred synthesized the conversation with a poignant question.

"By expressing my confidence in him and treating him as a valued partner, do you think he is motivated to be fully engaged with an *Us* mentality and encouraged to create as much value for *Us* as possible?"

"Absolutely!" Dusty stated with confidence. "I get that, but you still haven't addressed the issue of competition in a free market economy."

"Thanks for bringing me back to the question of competition, because this is a very important aspect of value creation. Competition in the marketplace is not only good, but necessary. However, the perspective you bring to all competitive endeavors is most critical. The distinguishing characteristic is whether you are competing *for* or competing *against* something and someone. I played football in high school and wanted to be the starting quarterback. I had a good friend who competed for the very same position.

"One day after practice we went to a local burger joint to talk – while we consumed some cheese fries and sodas. In that conversation we came to an understanding that safeguarded our friendship and inspired our play on the field. We agreed that we were not competing *against* one another. Instead we were competing *with* each other and *for* our team. We made a commitment to bring our best game to practice every single day so that we would push each other to get better. And then we would allow the coaches to decide which of us they felt could bring the most value to the team in each game situation. Our commitment was to give it our best shot and encourage one another in the process. By making that commitment, we both elevated our play *for* our own good and *for* the good of the team."

"So, who was chosen as the starting quarterback?" Dusty asked.

"It's funny that you should ask. I suppose I received more playing time, but there was something much larger at play than who took the first snap. You see, there were many times when he was tapped to lead the team when I got hurt or when his skill set better matched the game situation. We literally worked in tandem. The best part of it all was that he was my biggest fan and I was his. When I was leading the offense, he was watching the defense. Each time I came off the field, he would encourage me and tell me what he was seeing from his vantage point. He not only wanted me to play well, he gave me his best insight to ensure our victory. I will forever be marked by his example of humility. He put the interest of the team before his own and he inspired me to play at my best. To this day, we are still fast friends. And his example is one that I aspire to live out daily.

"I carried the lessons he taught me into the marketplace. I

was careful to make it clear to my senior leadership team that we were never to focus on comparing ourselves to other companies in our space. If you do that, there are only two possible outcomes. If you compare yourself to others and see yourself as better, then you fall prey to pride. On the other hand, if you come up short in the comparison, then you struggle with feelings of inferiority. Neither view is beneficial. Both rob you of the perspective necessary to bring your very best to play. Rather than defining success by comparing our work and outcomes to the accomplishments of others, we strove to pursue personal excellence. In this pursuit of excellence, we were comparing our performance and ourselves to our capabilities. We were intent on actualizing our potential through the creation of value.

"I also made it clear to our leaders that we would never view ourselves as competing *against* other companies in an attempt to put them out of business. Instead, our focus was on competing *for* the customer. Our objective was to create as much value *for* the customer as we possibly could in both product offerings and service. By doing so, our attitude was that we were competing *with* others to bring as much value to the market as possible, and we would let the customer decide who had the most to offer. That perspective, in and of itself, helped us to seize upon collaborative opportunities *with* others in our space and we formed a number of strategic alliances that created synergy and brought exponential returns. Many of those opportunities would have been missed had we adopted an antagonistic mindset of competing *against* others.

"Whenever we did go toe to toe with others in our space, we tried to do so with an attitude of humility that challenged everyone to create as much value *for* the customer as possible. Ultimately, the market decides who brings the most value. In the process, all players are challenged to elevate their games and the customer becomes the beneficiary of everyone's best efforts. Those who don't create value are eliminated. That is the essence of competitive markets," Fred concluded.

Dusty had never heard such a clear and concise explanation of competition in the marketplace. He had never thought about competing *for* the customer. He began to think about all the initiatives across the course of his career that had encouraged competition between business units. By leveraging the natural competitiveness of human nature, each initiative had set their own teams up to compete *against* one another in an attempt to improve performance. Now Dusty realized the foolishness of it all. What they had actually done was to create silos and establish unspoken game rules that impeded the sharing of best practices. After all, why would one team share the secret sauce with another team *against* whom they were competing? What they should have been doing all along was to reward those people and teams that were sharing best practices and inspiring others to create value by their example.

"So," Dusty summarized, "in each clutch situation, you have to decide whether you are going to *extract value* or *create value*. In doing so, you either put *I* over *Us* in an attempt to posture yourself to *extract value*. Or, you place *We* over *Me* as you begin to evaluate how you are going to *create value* for everyone involved."

"Correct," Fred affirmed. "If a person chooses to move with a mindset of extracting value, then a downward spiral is set in motion that will eventually lead to desperation. Let me describe to you how that happens."

Fred took the napkin from Dusty, flipped it over, and began to scribble on it again as he continued, "If someone places *I* over *Us*, then that person has chosen the path of value extraction, which is multiplied by the *ER* Factor.

$$\text{VALUE EXTRACTION} = I/US \times ER$$

The *ER* Factor is about competing *against* others and positioning self over others – the opposite of humility. *ER* stands for two components that are always prominent in value extraction:

Ego and *Rivalry*. A person's ego seeks to elevate self over others by trying to posture self as being smart-*ER*, fast-*ER*, strong-*ER*, and bright-*ER* – essentially bett-*ER* than others. This elevation of self immediately creates a competitive atmosphere where there is a clear winn-*ER* and a clear los-*ER* as that person tries to 'one up' everyone else. The *Rivalry* has begun. This *Rivalry* introduces another element that is even more crippling – pow-*ER*. Where there is opposition, the winn-*ER* is usually the one who is loud-*ER* and demonstrates more pow-*ER* than others involved. This 'powering up,' or escalation, is the antithesis of collaboration and involves self-promotion and dominance."

"Alright," Dusty interjected, before asking a clarifying question. "But isn't it sometimes necessary to exercise power when you meet resistance in order to move things forward?"

"Great question!" Fred responded. "Don't confuse power with influence. Leadership is about influence – inspiring people toward positive action. Power is about dominance – pushing others to action against their will. And remember the truism, 'Nothing of long-lasting positive value ever happens by force.' Influence, on the other hand, comes by modeling humility and living in growth gear. Living in growth gear, as we said, involves engaging with truth through honest evaluation and maintaining a solution-orientation. Demonstrating a willingness to change for the better inspires others to do the same.

"Those on the *ER* side of the situation demonstrate no real interest in personal growth. There is no vision for transforming the situation into something for the greater good of all. Rather, defensiveness takes over and individuals resort to *Rationalization* to justify their actions and attitudes. When people begin to rationalize behavior rather than facing it honestly and seeking to grow, *Stagnation* is the result. *Stagnation* occurs when there is no solution-orientation. In this state, collaboration and any movement toward a positive resolution are impeded. After awhile, people begin to pull away from one another. This *Alienation* creates an environment that is often characterized by *Desperation* – where a lack of trust forces people to act in self-protective ways. It is the exact opposite of what is created when people are in growth gear and an atmosphere of inspiration prevails. Choosing to extract value and placing *I* over *Us* is always compounded by *Ego* and *Rivalry*. You may get others to agree with you as you rationalize your behavior, but a positive outcome is all but impossible. No matter how many people may agree with you, the reality remains that bad choices have bad outcomes. Bad choices always have a *Gotcha!* And adopting a posture of value extraction is a bad choice."

Fred paused for a moment and then he summarized the downward spiral.

"Rather than getting into growth gear through honest evaluation, *Rationalization* disengages the gears of growth. *Rationalization* is the antithesis of authenticity. Rather than facing reality, a person makes excuses and justifies poor behavior. This inability to look at one's self honestly and the subsequent lack of ownership will eventually lead to *Stagnation*. As the situation degenerates, a lack of engagement prevents people from relating effectively or connecting deeply with each other. The emotional barriers erected through *Rationalization* to protect our egos are the very same barriers that prevent us from authentically connecting with others.

"This emotional distance causes *Alienation* from those with whom we need to connect in order to create value and positive movement. We find ourselves isolated from the very people with whom we long to connect. *Alienation* fosters *Desperation*. People begin to act out of self-interest rather than seeking what is mutually beneficial. Rather than growth, immaturity prevails. And it all begins with a choice to either *create value* or *extract value*. We have to consciously fight our selfish, instinctive tendency to *extract value*. We must remember in every clutch situation that bad choices always lead to bad endings. Always! Bad choices make bad situations worse – maybe not immediately, but ultimately! Bad choices will always find you out. Remember, 'Whatever is down in your well will eventually come up in your bucket."

Fred sat quietly for a moment and let Dusty process everything that he had said. Dusty stared at the napkin and thought through the progression. He had experienced the downward spiral both in his personal life and in organizational life. He could have given multiple examples to illustrate each of Fred's points. Yet, there was an opposition stirring within his spirit that he had to verbalize.

"So, let me press back for just a minute. Earlier you mentioned parenting issues. How would all of this relate to parenting? Do

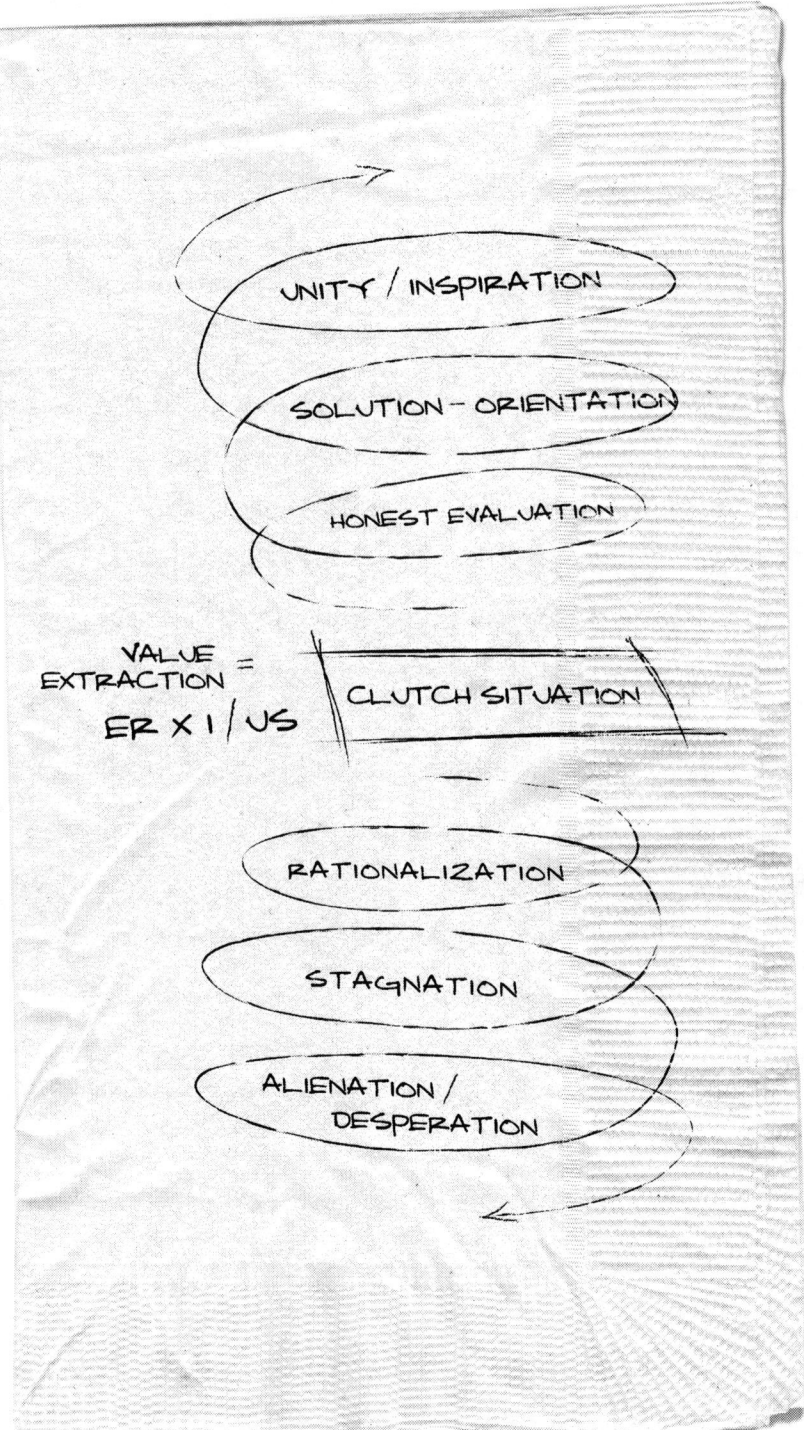

you believe that children should be given a choice? After all, the role of parents is to guide and direct their children's choices until they reach the point that they become responsible for their own choices. Children don't have a frame of reference large enough to make good choices."

"That is a great observation. Let me answer your question this way. The primary role of a parent is to help a child grow to maturity. Part of that process is learning to make good judgments, which result in good choices. Parents should give their children as many opportunities to make choices as they possibly can so that the choices themselves become a learning experience. Take the example of eating vegetables – something few children like to do. Should the parent allow the child to choose not to eat them, even though she knows how important it is for the child's health and growth? Obviously not! But, the parent can still allow the child to make a choice, once she has properly framed the options. Since not eating them is not a healthy option, the choice changes. What if the parent were to say something like, 'Johnny, vegetables are important for your growth and development. We want you to grow to be strong and healthy, so you get to choose which two vegetables you want to eat tonight. You don't have to eat a lot, but you do have to eat at least one serving of each. Then, if you are still hungry, you can choose to have seconds of whichever dish you wish. So, which two vegetables would you like?'

"The key," Fred continued, "is to offer a reasonable choice without allowing it to become a power struggle. You are the parent.

You are clearly in charge, but you want to allow Johnny to make his own choices so he can learn from each consequence and grow to make responsible decisions."

"Sure, but what if it does become a battle of the wills and little Johnny simply refuses to eat vegetables – period?"

"Then, you offer him another choice," Fred responded. "He can either choose to eat his dinner - including vegetables - with the family, or he can choose to go to his room alone without dinner. That way you aren't forcing him to eat vegetables. You are simply allowing him to make choices with some very clear consequences. He only has to choose the latter option once or twice and pretty soon he will figure out that going to bed hungry is far worse than holding his nose while eating a little squash. But, the choice is his and so are the consequences. He learns in the process."

"But, isn't that cruel and unusual punishment? Sending your child to bed hungry is pretty harsh," Dusty objected.

"Sometimes the choices we have to make in life *are* tough. Life would be pretty easy if our choices were limited to merely good versus bad or easy versus hard. The reality is that most of our choices in life come in the context of much more complicated valuation processes. Most choices we make in life present a conflict of values. And, every choice we make in life has consequences. Sometimes making the right choice and taking the necessary action needed to create the most value isn't always easy to swallow. But, the alternative is often an outcome that is even less palatable.

"There are times, of course, when you have to give directives and when you cannot afford to offer a choice. If someone demonstrates a lack of maturity to make responsible decisions in critical situations, then you are forced to become more direct in your guidance of that person. When the stakes are too high to take a chance on the outcome, then choices become limited. Let's say Johnny is chasing a ball into the street without stopping to look both ways for cars. That is no time to offer choices. In your loudest voice, you immediately bark a command in an authoritative tone that is unmistakable. There is no conversation or option – you expect immediate obedience! The stakes to do otherwise are simply too high. But most situations are not life and death. More often than not, looking for ways to offer choices will enhance the emotional buy-in of the other party."

Dusty was taking in everything Fred was saying like a sponge. This whole conversation about force and choice was resonating with him. He was ready to get more vulnerable and seek some personal advice. "So, Lisa and I have a 17-year-old son, Mike. We are really having a tough time with him right now. He's a good kid, but he's been copping an attitude recently. He is bright and talented, but not motivated to do his best work. To be blunt, he's lazy and a bit of a rebel. I have to ride him pretty hard to get him to pull things together. After all, it won't be long until he begins to apply to colleges and he has to get all of his ducks in a row if he wants to get into a good school. How would this all apply to Mike? If I'm not direct in guiding him and firm in my demands, then I fear he will slack off and squander away his future."

"What college does he want to attend?" Fred asked.

"We've visited five campuses, but haven't made any decisions. Right now, the plan is to apply to all five and see what responses we get."

"Great plan, but that wasn't the question. What school does *he* want to attend?"

"We want him to get into a school with a good MBA program. That way when he finishes his studies, he will be set for a nice future in business," Dusty offered.

"I'm not asking what *you* want. I am asking about what college *Mike* wants to attend. You see, herein lies the dilemma. What you want for Mike may not be what Mike wants for himself. If Mike wants it, he will work for it. If, on the other hand, he feels like he is only living out your dreams for him, then he has no opportunity to demonstrate mastery over his own thoughts and feelings. You are forcing your dream on him. He needs the freedom to pursue his own dream. He may conform for a season, but sooner or later he will resent it and rebel against what he feels is your pressure and your power to control his destiny. The reality is that your dream for him and his dream for himself may be one and the same, but he needs to be allowed to make that decision for himself. Only then will he be fully engaged and motivated to give the endeavor his best effort.

"Have you ever wondered why so many college freshmen literally throw away a semester or an entire year of educational opportunity by skipping classes or generally goofing off? Could it be that while they were at home so many decisions were made for them that they never learned to become responsible decision-makers? Or, maybe they were being forced to pursue courses of study at schools they were never genuinely interested in attending. Consequently, they didn't feel ownership of the choice or of their own lives because Mom and Dad were so heavily involved in the decision-making processes. Throwing away a good opportunity could be an expression of rebellion against a decision they felt helpless to make for themselves. They never really *owned* the decision, and therefore, never made a personal emotional investment in the outcome. They were neither encouraged nor equipped to live on purpose.

"Rather than telling Mike what he should want to do, why don't you help him set up some choices? Then, let him attempt to extrapolate those choices to a logical conclusion for himself. Eventually, Mike will begin to make responsible choices to reach his own goals. Help him think through the options as objectively as you possibly can without interjecting too much direct guidance, unless he asks for your input. *Remember, 'Unsolicited advice is rarely well received.'*

Unsolicited advice is rarely well received.

Making a decision of this magnitude is certainly important, but it's not the end-all of choices. If he chooses poorly, he can always transfer later to another school. And, if his course of study proves to be amiss, he can always change majors down the road. The point is that he is far more likely to take responsibility for the decisions he has the privilege of making. If you make the decision for him and it falls apart, he could always blame and resent you for a potentially bad outcome. That doesn't mean that you don't have high hopes and standards, or that you don't hold him accountable for being responsible. You express your deep belief in him and you encourage him to fulfill his potential. But remember, growth cannot be attained through force and manipulation. He has to fully own his decision and the resulting consequences. Owning the decision and taking responsibility for his actions is what we call maturity – or living on purpose."

Chapter Eleven

Responsibility

"Any discussion of maturity brings us to the fourth and final Maxim. The Maxim of Responsibility states that ***ownership empowers people to take responsibility for creating value,***" Fred explained. "Being value-centric means that in each and every clutch situation, you make choices that you believe will generate the most valucentricity. Then, you wholly own those decisions and act responsibly by taking the necessary action to create that value. In essence, you take ownership and responsibility for your choices. Again, it's an *EithER / OR* decision. In this case, *OR* is an acronym for *Ownership and Relationship*. *Ownership* means that an individual assumes responsibility for his decisions and actions. While *Relationship* implies a desire to stay engaged with others. An emphasis on *OR* leads to strong decision-making capability – *OR* is the

The Maxim of Responsibility

Ownership empowers people to take responsibility for creating value.

only path to empowerment.

"Let me ask you, Dusty, who has more vested interest in any business venture, the owner or the person he has hired to be the manager?" Fred queried.

"Obviously, the owner!"

"So, who is more likely to act responsibly and expend discretionary effort in making that business successful?"

"The owner," Dusty repeated.

"Right!" Fred responded. "Ownership carries a deeper sense of responsibility. In the same way, lots of folks talk about the need for adding value, but few are willing to take ownership and be responsible for creating the value they say they want. Even when people understand the power of these principles, they have to consciously choose to create value or they will be prone to follow their natural inclination toward a more selfish approach. What I am saying is that so much of this is counterintuitive. You see the tension each time a problem surfaces. Those who 'own' value creation jump in the fray and tackle tough issues. Those who prefer to 'manage' the situation will generally tend to distance themselves from anything that might disrupt the status quo.

"For any company, a primary consideration should always be, 'How do we structure our organization to allow everyone to think and act like owners?' When people feel that they 'own' the business, or at least a part of it, then they become more responsible for guarding the activity, resources and relationships in the business. Simply stated, where there is a sense of ownership, there is deeper emotional attachment. Ownership empowers people to take responsibility for creating value, thereby enhancing results.

Dusty thought for a moment about various members on his team and how some of them tended to respond in difficult situations when things drifted sideways or blew up altogether. Meetings that beckoned the question of responsibility for poor outcomes often looked like a fifth-grade sock hop. The music was playing, but nobody wanted to dance. In an attempt to avoid responsibility and possible rejection, everyone sat back and waited for someone else to make the first move. Nobody was willing to step up or step out on the dance floor. Instead, everyone tended to cluster around the safety of the punch bowl, so to speak, sipping the Kool-Aid. He wondered how much more productive they could have been had someone stepped up and assumed ownership of the situation rather than looking for ways to pass the buck. He mused for a moment about what might have been accomplished if only they had whole-heartedly applied their passion and strengths to solve the problem rather than emotionally distancing themselves and deflecting the issues onto others.

"Sorry," said Dusty, realizing his attention had strayed. "I got lost for a moment in my thoughts. I definitely see how this all plays itself out in real life. There is a stark contrast between *ER* and *OR*, isn't there?"

"Absolutely," Fred responded. "When you shift your thinking and put the emphasis on *OR*, it changes everything. Taking *Ownership* for your actions and seeking to strengthen *Relationships* in everything you do makes a world of difference. The emphasis shifts to doing what's right and what will bring the most value to life. It becomes less about *comparison* and more about *contribution*. It becomes less about *competition* and more about *collaboration*. And it is where you find fulfillment. It creates the ultimate win-win in each situation. Movements of good always begin with *OR* – *Ownership* and *Relationships*."

"In other words," Dusty interjected, "a person will seek to *eithER* protect and promote self and extract value from each situation, *OR* he will make choices to seek to serve others by bringing value to each situation. If someone seeks to extract value, then he places *I* over *Us* and everything becomes focused on *ER*. If, on the other hand, a person seeks to create value, then he places *We* over *Me* and moves forward with an attitude of *OR*, taking *Ownership* of his choices and strengthening *Relationships*. Essentially, *OR* multiplies your efforts to create value by plugging you into the power of valucentricity."

Fred smiled as he wrote on another napkin.

$$VC = WE/ME \times OR$$
$$2/1 = 2$$

"Now, watch the power of this idea," Fred continued, with a passionate tone in his voice. "In this formula, *VC* obviously stands for Value Creation. Watch what happens when *We* is placed over *Me* – you essentially get 2 over 1, or a total value of two. Now let's suppose you have a team of four people. When you place the good of the four and the contribution of 4 over the 1, then you get a total value of 4. The *VC* formula shows the power of multiplication. When leaders learn to empower their people and employ these principles, they leverage the power of multiplied effort and increase productivity exponentially. Valucentricity is generated. You can see how powerful this quickly becomes. When contributors all apply the *OR* Factor, substantial movements of good can be created.

"On the other side of every Clutch Situation is *VE*, or the Value Extraction Equation. By placing *I* over *Us*, you essentially get 1 over 2 or one-half. If the team in consideration is larger, then

$$VE = 1/US \times ER$$
$$1/5 = 20\%$$

the results are diminished proportionately. So, if you have five team members who are all seeking to extract value for themselves, then you essentially have 1 over 5, or 20 percent of the potential performance of their combined efforts. On the *VE* side people are divided and so is your effort. Essentially, you are unplugged from the power of valucentricity. Performance on the *VC* side is exponentially increased, while performance on the *VE* side diminishes rapidly," Fred concluded.

"So," Dusty interjected, "Value Creation multiplies your efforts, while Value Extraction divides both performance and people."

"Well said," affirmed Fred. "When you apply these formulas to teams, the negative and positive impacts can be stunning. Take an example from the world of sports. Do you remember the US Men's Basketball team of the 2004 Summer Olympics?" asked Fred.

"Of course I do," replied Dusty. "The team was stacked with

a bunch of young, talented players like Dwyane Wade, Carmelo Anthony and LeBron James. Then, you had two recent MVP's in Tim Duncan and Allen Iverson to round out the roster with what should have been another Dream Team."

"Right, but what happened?" asked Fred.

"They blew up. They literally imploded. They couldn't get their act together and play as a team. By all outward appearances, some of the players were more interested in making a name for themselves than in representing something larger – like the team or even the United States. It was embarrassing. They expected gold and barely walked away with the bronze medal. As a team, they were certainly divided and their efforts were diluted."

"No doubt about it! Now, do you remember the U.S. Ice Hockey team of the 1980 Winter Olympics?" asked Fred.

"Sure! When they beat the team from the Soviet Union it was dubbed 'The Miracle on Ice,'" offered Dusty.

"You know your sports," said Fred. "Up to that point, the Soviets had won nearly every world championship and Olympic tournament since 1954. *Sports Illustrated* touted the U.S. team victory as the 'Top Sports Moment of the 20th Century.' An inspirational and unconventional coach, named Herb Brooks, led them to defy the odds. But, here is a telling question. How many players can you name from that team?"

Dusty thought for a moment. No names readily came to mind. "I don't think I can name any of the players. I was pretty young in 1980," Dusty said in his defense.

"Of course you were. But isn't it interesting that you cannot name a single player from a match that was deemed the 'Top Sports Moment of the 20th Century?' That's because it wasn't about individual players. It wasn't about egos and spotlights. By his own assessment, Brooks was more interested in getting the right players than he was in getting the best players. When he brought them together, he challenged them to be bold and play for something greater than self. He focused all of their energy and effort on playing for each other and the country. And he inspired them to greatness. Together, they created a legacy that will long be remembered as individual credit paled in comparison to national pride."

Fred reflected for a moment as if giving homage to an honorable memory. Then he continued, "Every team or organization has a culture. Culture is nothing more than the collective expression of the values, thoughts and behaviors that individuals bring to the endeavor. Eith*ER* the culture will alienate teammates and divide and dilute effort, *OR* it will unify a team and multiply effort. You can have a culture by design or by default – either way, culture is paramount. A culture of value creation and multiplication is inspirational. A culture marked by alienation and division is usually characterized by desperation."

Dusty once again sat in silence, allowing the force of the formulas and their outcomes to ferment momentarily in his mind. It was becoming increasing clear to him just how impactful all of this could be on both a personal and a professional level. Finally, Dusty uttered simply, "Wow, this really is powerful stuff!"

EithER* the culture will alienate teammates and divide and dilute effort, OR *it will unify a team and multiply effort.

Chapter Twelve

The Question

"Let me remind you," Fred offered in summary, "that assuming ownership and making good choices isn't always as easy as it sounds. We have all been conditioned to one degree or another to protect and provide for ourselves first. This myopic, me-first mentality, flies in the face of value creation and makes valucentricity virtually impossible.

"In order to effectively confront this *I* over *Us* mentality, there are two issues to consider. First, we must focus on bringing the greatest value to everyone - not just self - that may be impacted by a decision. Such a decision-making process is others-focused. It's all about the *We*. There is another quote by Sir John Templeton that brings this into focus. He said, 'Never forget, the secret to creating wealth for oneself is to create it for others.' We benefit most by bringing value to others. And secondly, we must focus on long-term value generation versus the immediate benefit of any decision."

> **"Never forget, the secret to creating wealth for oneself is to create it for others."**
>
> Sir John Templeton

Dusty understood exactly what Fred was talking about. The sting of their earlier conversation about his son, Mike, had unmasked the fact that he was acting more in his own self-interest than he was in Mike's. There were un-denounced demons in his past that were driving him to react in ways that were counterproductive. He knew that, all too often, he had attached his own self-worth as a parent to Mike's performance. It was clear that his obsessive pushing of Mike to excel said more about his own insecurity than it said about his son. Dusty had come to realize through their conversation that he had not modeled for his son what it meant to live on purpose. Though he had good intentions, his own self-protective and self-promoting devices were skewing his ability to create real value for one of the most precious people in his life. Dusty knew, all too well, that many of his instantaneous reactions were creating no value. Quite the contrary, they were often relationally destructive. His need for control, which was an attempt to protect both his heart and his image, had caused strain in almost every close relationship in his life. It certainly had created negative repercussions in his relationships with Mike and Lisa.

"So how does someone stay focused on value creation in his thinking?" Dusty asked with all humility.

"That, my friend, is the issue that leads to the most impactful question," Fred responded. "In growing to become a value creation champion and coaching others to do the same, I have found it helpful to keep a guiding question front and center in my thinking. Every time I encounter a clutch situation, I always ask myself the same clutch question. Fred turned the napkin over and scribbled these words on the backside:

> THE CLUTCH QUESTION:
>
> WHAT'S THE SUPERIOR CHOICE?

"The Superior Choice is always the one that creates the greatest value. If I consciously ask myself this question in every situation, then I can hold my instinctive reactions at bay and make better decisions. The key is to pause and consider the options. Whether I am facing an important decision, engaged in a conversation or involved in a potentially volatile situation, I can act intentionally and live on purpose. Rather than being reactionary, I can respond in a manner that is consistent with my values. I can consciously make choices that have a much better chance of creating valucentricity.

"Let me explain what I mean with two real life examples," Fred continued. "Let's say I want to lose a few pounds. I know that to do so will require me to exercise regularly and watch what I eat. It's all about calorie intake and burn, right? So, I start regularly working out three days a week, walking and lifting weights. Now, with every meal, I have a choice to make. Either I will choose to eat foods that will sabotage my efforts, or I will make good choices that will create the greatest value. If I make poor choices regarding my food intake, I am minimizing the gains that I could be making through exercising regularly and eating healthily. As simple as that sounds, I am amazed how many people will rationalize a poor choice and label it a 'reward,' when the real reward of achieving greater value is being sabotaged. Will I justify poor choices or synergize my efforts with good choices? Rationalize or synergize – it's a choice.

"When I choose to live on purpose, I opt to live healthily. In making the decision to *be healthy*, many of my choices become crystal clear. The choice to *be healthy* impacts my food choices, my workout schedule, my sleep and my overall adequacy of self-care.

My values are aligned, producing valucentricity on a personal level.

"Another example is how we respond to others in the heat of the moment. Although Anne and I have been married for more than forty years, she would be the first to tell you that we have been *happily married* for somewhat less than forty years. How much less depends on the mood she is in when you ask her," Fred said with his usual grin.

"That is because I have not always applied the *OR* Factor in our marriage. Whenever Anne and I engage in a 'spirited discussion,' which is what I prefer to call a fight, I often allow my self-protective reactions to circumvent my conscious processes. The result is that I react in some very unpleasant ways. Consequently, I have spent more nights in the guest room than I care to admit. Through practice, I have learned – admittedly, all too slowly – how to stop myself from reverting back to old patterns of communication. Whenever the conversation turns 'spirited,' I ask myself *The Clutch Question* – What is the Superior Choice? Then, I can take *Ownership* of my choices and make the *Relationship* my higher priority. I have found that when the *OR* Factor is applied in any situation, in business or personal life, it really works. Rather than being reactive to the situation, I become proactive by making choices that produce the greatest value. I engage in the process of *Evaluation* to seek a *Solution* that can lead toward an *Inspirational* conclusion – both of us wanting to be better."

While Fred was talking, Dusty's mind wandered to numerous encounters with Lisa when he had immediately become defensive when she had expressed even the slightest disappointment in him. Why did he instinctively do that? Did he have a deep-seated need to manage his image or protect a tender ego? Why did he deflect responsibility rather than take ownership of anything that might reflect poorly on him? He clearly saw how he lived out the downward spiral, making matters worse. It had always frustrated Dusty how the smallest of issues frequently turned into knockdown, drag-out fights. All too quickly, conversations could turn into arguments, leaving them shouting from opposite sides of the room. At times, they could hardly stand to be in each other's presence. He certainly wasn't thinking of creating value in those clutch situations.

In each heated exchange, he had been more interested in maximizing Lisa's faults and minimizing his own. Now, he saw that approach as nothing more than a feeble attempt to rationalize his behavior. Dusty began to see just how proficient he had become in utilizing a wide array of excuses to deflect any personal responsibility. Rather than making the Superior Choice to create value, he had often turned the conversation around to cast a shadow of blame on Lisa, alienating her and creating a desperate situation. He wondered how very different things might have been in each of those scenarios if he had simply asked himself *The Clutch Question* and made a Superior Choice to create value.

Caught up in his own thoughts, his facial expression must have betrayed him.

"Are you all right?" asked Fred.

The Question

"Oh, I'm fine. It's just that this all hits a little too close to home – no pun intended. I was just thinking of a myriad of situations with Lisa in which I have failed to create value. I am afraid I have really blown it," Dusty humbly admitted.

"Yes, you have!" Fred said with a wry smile and a sarcastic tone. "And so has everyone else on the planet. One thing I learned a long time ago is that the more personal you think something to be, the more universal it actually is. Dusty, the fact is that we have all blown it. That is why this is so profound. The only way to reverse the damage done is to change the pattern of behavior by applying these principles of value creation and making Superior Choices," Fred said.

He let the thought hang in the air like a fragrant perfume. After a long pause, Fred continued.

"In simply stopping to ask *The Clutch Question*, there is a progression that takes place that is important to note. The mental progression of making Superior Choices begins with *consideration* – slowing long enough to stop oneself from reacting in any situation and taking time to consider the possibilities. This prevents a knee-jerk reflex. I can literally stop myself from reacting and being driven by my self-protective devices. The ancient word 'sider,' which is where we get the word consider, literally means 'wisdom.' When I stop to consider the options and their possible consequences, I am thinking wisely. The next step in the progression is *valuation*, or evaluation – the weighing of those options. I want to give significance or weight to each option according to my value system

— what I deem to be most important. By doing this, I place greater value on one thing over another. At this point, I am pondering what decision will lead to the greatest long-term value. Then, I commit to the best option and take *action*. Actions speak louder than intentions. Actions speak louder than goals. Actions are the only true reflection of commitment. Your actions, not your words, will reveal the true condition of your heart and mind."

"Or you could say," Dusty interjected playfully, "Whatever is down in your well will eventually come up in your bucket!"

"Whatever is down in your well will eventually come up in your bucket!"

"Well said," Fred affirmed. "It's all about making the Superior Choice. By taking *Ownership* of the choice and focusing on what's best for the *Relationship*, we are plugging into the power of valucentricity."

"You've used the phrase 'the greatest long-term value' a couple of times now. I think I know what you mean, but I would like for you to explain the concept a little more," Dusty said.

"Happy to," Fred replied. "I'm glad you brought me back around to this because it's the second element that must be considered in making the Superior Choice. Each time we make a decision, there is a short-term and a long-term dimension that must be considered. Many people only make decisions based upon the short-term outcomes. Many decisions have a short-term gain but carry a long-term loss – while other decisions may have a short-term loss, but ensure a long-term gain. When faced with the choice, many people opt for the short-term benefit and forfeit the potential to create greater value in the long run. Let me show you what I mean.

"Anne and I just moved into a garden home. With the kids grown and gone, we didn't need the big house anymore. So we sold it and moved into something smaller. I have the time and I enjoy being outdoors, so I decided to start doing the yard work again for myself. The problem was that I had no equipment. I picked up a nice used lawnmower at a garage sale, but I needed an edger. I went to the local home and garden store and started looking at the options. In addition to the basic tools, they had some really cool, top-of-the-line, new-fangled, and high-powered stuff with all the bells and whistles.

"As I was drooling over the equipment, a young sales associate approached and asked if he could help me. He could tell right away that I was a pushover. I was practically selling myself on the most expensive edger in the line. He could have agreed with me and sold me that edger, but he didn't. Instead, he asked why I needed an edger. When I explained that my yard was extremely small and my needs were meager, he suggested two other options at a much lower price point. He was down-selling me on an affordable option that fully met my needs. He could have sold me the more expensive edger and benefited in the short-term. However, if I got home and experienced buyer's remorse over having purchased something I really didn't need, he could very likely have had a disgruntled customer who might never return to the store.

"Fortunately, I came to my senses and realized that he was right. I could have easily paid four times the price for something I never would have needed. But, he chose to create the greatest value for me, the customer. He actually took a short-term loss – a lesser sale than he could have made. But, in doing so, he received a long-term gain – he made me a customer for life. He gained my trust and loyalty. Now, every time I go back to that store I ask for the same sales associate. I would dare say that I have spent a small fortune on home repairs with him serving as my advisor.

Many decisions have a short-term gain, but carry a long-term loss; while other decisions may have a short-term loss, but ensure a long-term gain.

"Now, let me take that same thought and apply it to my relationship with Anne. If she comes at me aggressively in one of our lively conversations, I could choose the short-term benefit of defending and justifying my actions. In that moment, it may feel good and appropriate to prove myself right, but in the long-term it could cost me much more relationally. On the other hand, adopting a humble attitude and asking her to show me my shortcomings may feel like death in the short-term. But in the long-term, that kind of humility let's her know that I am placing *We* above *Me* and that I want to learn how to create as much value in our relationship as possible for *Us*."

Fred took a deep breath and let the pregnant pause allow time for Dusty's thoughts to gestate. Dusty looked at the napkin with *The Clutch Question* written on it. He couldn't believe that such a small piece of recycled paper could contain so much wisdom. If that simple question could be understood and applied, he knew it could radically change his personal life and the way he conducted business – for good.

Dusty thanked Fred for his time and the two men parted company. Dusty had a lot to do to prepare his presentation for the Engagement Task Force. His head was flooded with ideas about how they might craft an approach that would create the greatest value for their customers and team members. All day Friday and through the weekend, Dusty pored over his notes and did more research.

Dusty crafted a deployment proposal that included a series of workshops, each designed to teach team members the Maxims of Value Creation. He decided to follow up these workshops with a series of short, high-impact online coaching videos that were designed to reinforce the principles taught in the workshops. He thought this form of "drip development" would be well received since it did not require taking team members offline for long periods of time. These video segments would expose them to terse, transformational content in bite-sized coaching editions that could be applied easily. It was all coming together.

By midday on Monday, Dusty was armed and ready to make his presentation to the Task Force. That night he was like a kid before Christmas. He couldn't remember when he had been so excited about the potential outcome of a presentation. He could hardly sleep as he kept imagining the flow of the meeting the following morning. The funny thing was that his excitement had less to do with his presentation as it did with what he imagined could be the start of a corporate cultural transformation. If everyone understood and applied the principles of value creation, it truly could be revolutionary. The night was short but restful.

The next morning, Dusty was anxious to get to work. He actually noticed that he had a genuine spring in his step and a brighter attitude as he walked into the office. He could hardly wait to see what opportunities the day would present. And he knew that in every clutch situation he would be asking himself, "*What Superior Choice will produce valucentricity?*"

SECTION FOUR

ADVANCEMENT

Chapter Thirteen

Transformation

As the members of the Task Force started to gather, Dusty looked out the windows of the conference room on the sixteenth floor. The panoramic view of the city was breathtaking. A storm had gathered clouds over the city and was threatening to bring heavy rains. But on the horizon, the morning sun was breaking through the heavy clouds and throwing beams of light to the ground in a stunning display of contrast. Dusty seized upon this amazing visual and used it as a metaphor to begin the meeting.

"According to the data, less than a third of the American workforce could be described as 'Actively Engaged,' meaning that they bring enthusiasm, passion and creativity to the work experience. More than half of the workforce is 'Not Engaged,' with about twenty percent being 'Actively Disengaged.' According to many experts, the figure for lost productivity due to a non-engaged workforce is estimated to be around $350 billion a year in the United States alone. This lack of emotional attachment to work leads to low morale, lack of loyalty, sparse innovation, and less than stellar performance. Though this dark cloud threatens to rain on our efforts, I believe we have the opportunity and the resources necessary to shine a light that is as bright and beautiful as the one you can see on the horizon," Dusty said as he pointed out the window. The introduction was providential, he thought to himself. Not a bad way to start the meeting.

Then, he set up the conversation about the Maxims of Value Creation by showing them a formula that he had come across in his reading. He felt it vividly illustrated the issues at play. Dusty wrote the formula on the white board:

$$\triangle \text{behavior} = \triangle \text{results}$$

"The deltas represent change," Dusty said as he teed up the presentation. "If you want to change the results, then you have to change the behaviors that produce those results. Many folks might call this behavior modification. So, if company B wants to get the same results as company A, they may analyze and attempt to emulate the policies, procedures and processes employed by company A. The problem, however, is that it rarely produces the same results. This is because the behavior of company A is driven by a way of thinking that causes them to act in a certain way. For those who are smart enough to recognize this reality, they may pursue a wide array of training initiatives to reframe the way folks think about their environment and how they process information. This is what psychologists would call cognitive therapy. It is an attempt to help people see life and activities from a different and hopefully more productive vantage point. And, as such, it can have a positive impact upon behavior and ultimately productivity.

$$\triangle \text{ thinking} > \triangle \text{ b} = \triangle \text{ r}$$

"But if you really want to create long-lasting positive change, then you have to know what drives the thinking behind the behaviors, which produce the results. That element, which is foundational to both our thinking and our behavior, is our value system. Values create the grid through which our thoughts, decision-making processes and performance are all integrated. So, if you want to change the results, it's not enough to change the behavior, or even the thinking behind the performance. To have long-lasting positive results you, have to assess and align the values, which give rise to the thinking, which produces the behavior, that garners the results. In effect, this is the *Formula for Cultural Transformation*. When values are aligned, then thinking is enhanced, and behaviors are inspired to achieve superior results.

Value Alignment > △ t > △ b = △ R

"What we need to do to reach our full potential is to allow our values to drive our business. We need to define, articulate, and embody our values. We need to select people whose values align with the values of those who comprise the organization. And, we need to reinforce the principles of value creation in everything that we do if we want better results."

Dusty paused for a moment to assess everyone's body language. He wanted to make sure that everyone was engaged. And from what he could sense, he definitely had their attention. But before he could continue the presentation, there was a question.

Dan, a key influencer on the team pointedly asked, "So, how do you judge whether or not someone has strong values. Couldn't it get rather dicey if we begin to claim that we can accurately assess someone's morals or character?"

"That's a great question," Dusty responded. "Let me clarify the concept. When I say 'values,' I am referring to how people evaluate certain aspects of the world around them. A person's values determine the way in which an individual views the world and interprets activity in his environment. Values are shaped by how much importance an individual places upon certain elements in a decision-making process. This way of viewing certain dimensions of life and work has as much to do with functionality and productivity as it does with ethics and morality.

"For instance, if I were to ask you if you value safety, I am sure that everyone in this room would answer with a resounding 'Yes.' If I were to ask you if speed and efficiency are important, you would also likely respond in the affirmative. But what happens if I place you in a situation where it is impossible to complete a task on schedule while also taking the time necessary to adhere to an agreed upon set of procedures to ensure safety? Which gets the short end of the stick? Do you complete the task on time, while demonstrating risky behavior? Or, do you place safety above meeting the deadline? Either way, you have just made a valuation – a decision based upon what you value more. Neither choice speaks to your morality. Such a process of evaluation has more to do with effectiveness than it does with ethics, but it deals with your values nonetheless. Such a decision shows clearly whether safety or timeliness is more highly valued.

"The problem is that many companies do not clarify what is of greater importance. They say that both are vital and leave it up to the individual to make a determination in the moment. In doing so, the organization sets everyone up for frustration. There will always be those who will err on the side of timeliness and others who will choose to err on the side of safety. Therefore, it leaves a cloud of confusion. Without clarity anyone can find himself wedged between a rock and a hard place, unable to get unstuck because he is being pulled in two opposing directions.

"But, suppose that same organization takes a firm stand on the side of safety over speed. That is not to say that they disregard the importance of deadlines, but they make it clear that if it ever comes to one over the other, then they will always choose safety first. Now it is clear where they stand. When it comes to the issue of safety, they can live it, hire to it, teach it, and reinforce it to make sure that everyone is on the same page. In essence, they can assess and align the organization around safety as a key value. They can begin to build a culture around safety. There is no confusion around this issue. It is clear – safety first!

"Now suppose that within that same culture, you still have individuals who skirt safety procedures for the sake of efficiency. They may very well be good, moral people with a strong work ethic, but they are risk-takers who are willing to forgo certain procedures in order to get more work done. What do you do with those otherwise productive folks? If you let them continue without intervention, you jeopardize your reputation as a safe company and other team members will begin to question whether or not safety is a real value. Assessment and alignment is the key. They must be groomed to understand that when safety and timeliness conflict, then safety must come first. With that clearly established, then people either choose to adopt safety as the superior value or find themselves in direct conflict with the organizational culture. Where there is no clear value alignment, then the organization is reduced to a police state – enforcing adherence to certain behaviors. Where there is alignment, unity, harmony and productivity prevail. Alignment produces valucentricity – the flow of energy that comes through synergy."

Dusty could tell that what he was saying resonated with the team. He had everyone's full and undivided attention. A few heads were even nodding in agreement, so he continued.

"Value adoption cannot be forced. Values are always chosen on a personal level. It is a truism that, *'Nothing of long-lasting positive value ever happens by force.'* Forced compliance never leads to healthy collaboration – you get a warped culture instead. Where values are misaligned, you have a culture by default rather than by design. But when a group decides collectively what is highly valued, and you have alignment across the organization, then remarkable movements of good can come out of such clarity."

Dusty took a deep breath and let the significance of what he had just said sink in for a moment. Then, he summarized his thoughts before opening the floor for discussion.

"The only real competitive advantage any organization has is the culture that it fosters. Culture is really nothing more than the composite of the values, thoughts and behaviors of the individuals who comprise any organization. Culture, then, is the collective expression of individual values. Companies do not possess values – people do. Crafting a values statement and prominently hanging it in the lobby is nothing more than an aspirational activity if the people in the life of the organization do not embody those values. But when the values of the people are clearly aligned with the direction and commitment of the organization, then a culture is crafted where people are free to express their passion, use their gifts and fulfill their potential in creating value. In essence, the culture of an organization can be impacted positively by taking action to assess and align values. Rather than being aspirational, aligned values can truly become transformational.

"Where the culture is strong, it becomes possible to create movements of good. And those movements of good become the Superior Advantage. A culture, which creates movements of good will be characterized by trust and unity. In this superior culture, synergy replaces silos. Competition is minimized and collaboration becomes the norm. And, last but not least, individual self-promotion is marginalized in the shadow of collective value creation and celebration. A company's culture is the engine that generates the power to drive movements of good. A healthy corporate culture will create value for everyone.

"When a company experiences clear values alignment, they embody their values. They hire to them, coach to them, and reinforce them throughout the organization. And, when everyone is on the same page, you have successfully crafted a Remarkable

Culture where people BELIEVE the best *IN* each other; WANT the best *FOR* each other and EXPECT the best *FROM* each other."

Where the culture is strong, then it becomes possible to create movements of good. And those movements of good become the Superior Advantage.

Having framed the conversation, Dusty and Jim Mitchell co-led the rest of the meeting. Dusty presented the Maxims of Value Creation and explained what it meant to live on purpose. There was much discussion. Everyone was fully engaged in the process. Ideas were bouncing around the room like popcorn heated in an open container. The meeting was scheduled to last until noon. It was so productive, however, that everyone agreed to clear their afternoon calendars and have lunch brought in.

The team was captivated by the maxims and how they might be applied to impact performance in positive ways. The concept of empowerment was not new to anyone, but the succinct manner in which Dusty had so clearly articulated and applied it was refreshing. Dusty could not remember a time when there had been so little conflict and so much collaboration in a meeting of leaders. Even when impassioned challenges or penetrating questions arose, Dusty found himself addressing each with less defensiveness, while relying upon *The Clutch Question* to center his thinking on value creation. It truly was one of the most productive meetings he had ever experienced at Query – or in his career for that matter. Time literally flew. Finally, late in the afternoon, Jim had to bring closure to the meeting.

As the meeting concluded, Jim approached Dusty. With a smile as wide as the Mississippi River, he patted Dusty on the back and simply said, "Well done!"

Dusty knew in that moment he had begun a process that had the potential to bring great value to the organization. Collectively, they had the opportunity to create a movement of good like none they had ever seen. He knew it would be a process. It wouldn't happen overnight. But he was excited about what the future could hold for him and his teams as they sought to create value for their clients, one another and ultimately for the company. He was energized, optimistic, and hopeful. His passion had been renewed.

Formula for Cultural Transformation

$$VA > \triangle t > \triangle b > \triangle R$$

When values are aligned, then thinking is enhanced and behaviors are inspired to achieve superior results.

Chapter Fourteen

Resistance

Dusty and Fred met weekly while Query was in the early stages of deployment of what the leadership team called the *VC Initiative*, with its accompanying workshops and "drip development." For the most part, the work had been received with rave reviews. However, there were pockets of resistance and a few negative voices that frankly caught Dusty by surprise. Of course he knew that any initiative would be met with some measure of resistance, but the feedback from the few was disheartening nonetheless. Being the recovering perfectionist and control freak that he was, the negativity of the minority began to get under his skin. Like termites embedded in the support beams of a house, they began to eat away at the core of his confidence in what the team was attempting to build. He was worried that the presence of such negativity might stifle their ability to create the kind of culture that he was beginning to dream was possible.

A particularly painful encounter came when he was blindsided by one of his direct reports and team leads named Lanny. Dusty had always maintained an open-door policy. Mirroring that attitude, he only closed his door when he needed privacy or did not want to be distracted, while working on a project. Late one afternoon, Lanny knocked on the open door of his office.

"Come on in, Lanny. What can I do to create value for you this afternoon?" Dusty asked.

"Dusty, I just need to talk. I don't know that I am fully on board with all of this value creation stuff. I mean, I don't understand exactly what I am supposed to be asking my people to do. There are few metrics to monitor progress and no objective standards to which I can hold my people accountable. I am having a hard time wrapping my head around how I am expected to lead my team in this initiative if there aren't specific goals that we are driving."

Dusty thought he might understand why Lanny was having such a tough time. Initially, it was hard for him to grasp as well. After all, it was difficult to create a checklist that, when completed, was guaranteed to produce value. Furthermore, how could value creation be objectively measured anyway?

Lanny had a military background and had attained the rank of colonel before retiring from the service and entering the civil sector. He was a respected leader and a top performer who had been tapped to oversee a floundering operations team. He had taken a lackluster, undisciplined team and turned it around by applying additional metrics to monitor progress and timetables that exceeded the company's expectations. Every goal was broken down into objectives and every objective had its action items with deadlines. By all accounts, Lanny was a gentle giant. But it was clear that top performance for him was equated with strict adherence to rigid guidelines with little room for personal expression.

Lanny's team was productive, but Dusty always felt they lacked passion. A walk through the cubicle landscape of his team and one noticed right away that it looked like a barracks at boot camp. Every desk was clutter-free. There were very few personal items in each work space and cork boards were filled with graphs and charts. The overall tone throughout the space could easily have been mistaken for a wake. Collegial conversation was noticeably absent. Everyone actively participated in "the drill," but there was very little camaraderie. When five o'clock rolled around each day, it appeared as if everyone had gone AWOL in his unit. If any team needed to understand and apply the Maxims of Value Creation, it was Lanny's team, Dusty thought to himself.

Lanny was all about driving business. He was a true tactician. It wasn't that Lanny lacked a genuine concern for his team members. It was more that he felt someone's personal life should never interfere with his professional performance. He believed firmly that you have your personal life on the one hand and your professional life on the other – and never the two should meet. Therefore, he never made an attempt to get to know what his team member's lives were like outside the office. They really didn't know much about his either. And, he liked it that way. There was a secure, non-emotional, neutral zone between the home and the office. It made his work as a leader much more objective, or so he thought.

"Dusty," he continued, "all of this emphasis on positivity is a bit too touchy-feely for me. How do you hold someone accountable for creating value? It's all too philosophical and fluffy. As for all this talk about passion and leveraging strengths, what does that have to do with business? My team is only as strong as its weakest link. Everyone in my charge had better be proficient in all aspects of the work or I'm a poor leader. If a single team member isn't prepared or alert, then the entire team's productivity could be compromised. That is why I work so hard to cross-train and regularly assess each team member to make sure there are no glaring deficiencies."

"Lanny, there is no doubt in anyone's mind that you have done a stellar job in meeting your business objectives. Your team has exceeded just about every metric that we have put in place to drive productivity. But do you ever wonder if your people really enjoy their work?"

"May I be direct?" Lanny asked.

"Of course you can," responded Dusty.

"Dusty, frankly it's not about enjoyment. The way I see it, if my team members are receiving a paycheck twice a month from this organization, then they had certainly better be 'engaged' in their work," Lanny said as he made quotation marks in the air with his fingers. "It's not about personal satisfaction – it's about fulfilling their duty. I agree with the principle of taking responsibility for your actions. It is the responsible thing to do the work that you are paid to do – period!"

Dusty admired Lanny's work ethic. He was able to turn a floundering team around by establishing drills and discipline. But he certainly would not describe Lanny's team as flourishing – even though their numbers were impressive. He wondered how long many of them would stay with the organization if given an opportunity to go elsewhere.

"Lanny, let me ask the same question another way. Imagine for a moment that you had no corporately bestowed authority, no title, and no officially appointed position. What if you had no ability to remunerate or reprimand the members of your team? Imagine that you had nothing but your values and a mission. How many of the folks in your charge would show up tomorrow simply because they believe in you as the leader and in the mission of the organization? How many of your team members possess a deep sense of purpose and passion for what they do? In other words, are they emotionally invested in the work?"

The more our values are in alignment as a team, the more value we can create for everyone. Unity is a powerful force in driving productivity.

Lanny sat in stunned silence. The expression on his face reflected his bewilderment. Dusty continued to drive the point.

"Don't you serve on the board of The Rescue Mission?" Dusty asked Lanny.

"Yes, for almost five years now."

"Picture that group, or any one of a number of not-for-profit organizations. They all do good work and have a number of committed volunteers. Those volunteers give their time and energy without receiving any payment. Why? They do it because they believe in the cause. They are aligned with the values and the vision of the organization. They receive something in return that is a greater motivator than money. They are led by passion and purpose. Of course, we are a for-profit organization. We do have the ability to reprimand and remunerate. But I often wonder how much more innovative and productive we could be if our people possessed that same kind of passion for their work. Lanny, I deeply believe that kind of passion has everything to do with someone's ability to live on purpose and create value. The more our values are in alignment as a team, the more value we can create for everyone. Unity is a powerful force in driving productivity. And I am asking you to throw your influence into this initiative. Even if it doesn't all make sense to you right now, will you at least agree that the two of us can keep talking it through?"

Lanny took a moment to reflect without responding, the question hanging in the air like smoke from a dry cigar. Then with measured words he finally spoke, "Dusty, I will commit to keep an open mind and a conversation going with you. But, I will be candid and I will not mince words. You will not have to guess where I stand. If I begin to feel that this is all bunk, you will know it from me."

"That's all I can ask right now," Dusty responded. "But, don't wait for me to find you. If there is something on your mind that you want to talk about, you know where to find me. Let's keep the conversation going about how we can make this practical and meaningful."

As Dusty watched Lanny leave the office, he couldn't help but wonder where this all was going to lead. He knew that organizationally they were on the right path. He also knew that each team member would have to make a personal choice to follow that path. Dusty had come to understand that choices were a vital part of the maturation process. Each time he began to feel the angst rise within him, he fought off the tendency to power up and issue directives. Rather than resort to his normal reactive ways, he would remind himself that, '*Nothing of long-lasting positive value ever happens by force.*'

Chapter Fifteen

Remarkable

Thursday afternoon when they met at the coffee shop, Dusty skipped the cordial small talk and immediately started firing questions at Fred.

"So, how do you handle resistance? What do you do when people drag their feet and challenge the basic premises of value creation? And, more importantly, how do you hold people accountable while attempting to create this kind of cultural transformation?"

"Those are great questions! Which leg of the skunk do you want to pull first?" Fred responded calmly with a deadpan look on his face.

"Let's talk about dealing with resistance first," Dusty chimed in. "It drives me crazy when people attempt to sink ideas or initiatives before they ever give them a chance to float. In the break room at work, we have a framed picture of a sailing vessel with a caption underneath that reads, 'In order to discover new worlds, you have to lose sight of the shore.' It is an obvious encouragement to be bold and courageous. But too many people are frankly just cowards when it comes to change. We will never get out of the port if people start blowing holes in the bottom of the boat before it ever gets into deep water. The irony of it all is that the hole-punchers are actually *on the boat*. As long as we are bailing water while in the shallows, we are never going to discover new worlds. How do you deal with those who want to swamp the boat before it gets out of the bay?" Dusty asked, with a distinct tone of agitation.

"Why does opposition surprise you, Dusty? This isn't your first voyage. You know there will always be some measure of resistance to change. Some people struggle with it more than others. You will always have early adopters and those who are cynical and resistant."

"You're right, but I am surprised by some of the folks who just don't seem to get it. What do you do with people who choose to be negative?"

"In your question, you have your answer," Fred said, stopping Dusty midstream.

"What do you mean?" asked Dusty.

"You said, 'people who choose to be negative.' They are making a choice. They are choosing to remain on the dark side. And, every choice has consequences. Dusty, let me be blunt and cut to the chase. There are three types of people that will rapidly deplete the energy of any organization. Those three types of people are the

Victims, the *Naysayers*, and the *Know-It-Alls*."

Fred paused to take a long, slow drink from his cup of raspberry tea. He savored the blend for a moment as if to draw additional strength before engaging in a draining conversation. Then, with reflective resolve he continued.

"Victims are people who view problems as personal persecution rather than impersonal challenges to overcome. They walk through life waiting for the anvil to fall. They are often angry, usually annoyed and almost always complaining about having been taken advantage of by someone. For them, the world is not safe and people cannot be trusted. *Victims* see problems in every opportunity. They look for and attract others who feel they have been treated unjustly. Ultimately, *Victims* are self-destructive. They live out negative self-fulfilling prophesies that are deeply rooted in their own sense of unworthiness. Don't get me wrong, we all can see ourselves occasionally as *Victims*, but chronic *Victims* have chosen to turn their negative view of the world into a way of life. The saddest part is that they seem to enjoy playing the role of the *Victim*. That's probably because they can evoke sympathy from others by recounting their sad stories. That is, until they begin to drain the lifeblood out of everyone around them. They are emotional black holes, sucking the positive energy out of everything and everyone they touch."

"I know the type," Dusty chimed in. "At first, you want to help. But, after awhile, you begin to realize that life for them is a non-stop series of crises. What about the *Naysayers*?"

"*Naysayers* are those individuals who are perpetually pessimistic. Nothing is ever good enough. Nothing will ever work. Nothing you or anyone else can do will ever get them to see the brighter possibilities in life. *Naysayers* are the Eeyore's of life. You remember Eeyore, the character from *Winnie-the-Pooh*? He is the old gray stuffed donkey who mopes around, speaking monotone and casting a negative pall over everything. He lives in the southeast corner of the Hundred Acre Wood, in an area labeled 'Eeyore's Gloomy Place.' He lives in a stick house, which collapses quite often. He thinks poorly of most of the other animals in the forest. And, of course, Eeyore's favorite food is thistles, which speaks volumes."

"*Naysayers* block progress. They may claim to be realists, but they are not. A realist sees a situation for what it is, but can still be vibrantly optimistic. *Naysayers* highlight the negatives and doubt the possibilities. *Naysayers* use the darker crayons in the box to color life, and they generally can be characterized as gloomy, pessimistic, and depressing. *Naysayers* are fools that cannot be convinced that there is any other way to see the world. Dark lenses cloud their world-view. They are momentum killers and a cancer to any organization."

"And," Dusty interjected, "just like the *Victims*, *Naysayers* end up fulfilling their own negative prophesies. It's sort of like what Henry Ford said, 'Whether you think you can, or you think you can't – you're right.' Because they think negatively, for them, it cannot be done."

"Right," Fred affirmed. "But here is a kicker – in spite of their negativity, *Naysayers* can be hard workers. The problem, however, is that for all of their work, they create very little true value. Rather than developing a sense of self-worth by creating value, their identity is often defined by what they are against. On the surface, they may give the impression of having a strong work ethic. They may possess passion and pursue a cause with intensity. But, you have to understand what drives them. *Naysayers* are fighters. As long as you align with their view of reality, then they can be fierce defenders and soldiers in arms. But the minute you oppose them, they can turn on you and fight against you with the same intensity that they have demonstrated toward other 'enemies.'"

Dusty began to think of people along his career path that were the epitome of what Fred had just characterized as the *Naysayers*. He remembered vividly a number of debates where he had attempted to convince a *Naysayer* of the value of a project or direction. He recalled how frustrated and exhausted he felt on the backside of those nonproductive, point/counterpoint conversations. *Naysayers* could deadlock most any conversation, initiative, or project until the stalemate would eventually have to be broken with an edict.

Even then, the grumblers might hold out in the deployment phase. There might be concession and compliance, but very little discretionary effort exerted to guarantee the success of the work. They have no concept of the *OR* Factor, Dusty thought. Bringing Dusty back from his momentary mental excursion, Fred continued as he turned his attention to the *Know-It-Alls*.

"And then we have the *Know-It-Alls*," Fred said with a deep sigh. "A *Know-It-All is* smarter than everyone else on the team, at least in his opinion of himself. You may have heard it said that, 'leaders are learners.' Well, a *Know-It-All* can never be a true leader. In his own estimation, he has little left to learn. He is the expert on everything. He purports to be a leader, but very few follow. When he walks out of the room, others roll their eyes. He cannot engender trust because he lacks humility. A *Know-It-All* is constantly trying to position himself as the turn-to-guy who has all the answers. The interesting thing is that if you watch closely, rarely does anyone turn to him to seek his advice. Nonetheless, he will offer his opinion on just about any topic anyway. Do you remember when I told you that unsolicited advice is rarely welcomed? Well, the *Know-It-All* hasn't figured that out yet."

By this point Dusty was a full sponge. He had absorbed so much that he was beginning to leak. With each description, he had envisioned team members who were guilty on all counts. He could no longer contain his frustration. "So what am I supposed to do? I can't just waltz into the office on Monday morning and start doling out reprimands and pink slips. And besides, why have I not noticed all of these behaviors before now?"

"Why don't we take those questions in reverse order," Fred suggested. "Could it be that the reason you haven't noticed these behaviors until now is because you have created what I call a Directive Culture? Your work environment tends to lend itself toward a leadership model that doesn't allow for much freedom of expression or creativity. In other words, very little discretion is needed. Decisions are all dictated for team members. And, consequently, there is little true ownership. People are going through the motions to hit the numbers and fill in the blanks. But, that's about it. There is little room for creativity or what might begin to lean into innovation.

"But now, you are talking about living on purpose and encouraging people to use their passion and strengths in new and creative ways to maximize productivity. You are allowing them to make their own choices, which is the only way that you can get to discretionary effort. But the flip side is that in making those choices, you actually may be seeing their true dispositions for the first time. What may have been suppressed in a more mandated environment is beginning to surface as you pursue more purposeful value creation."

"That makes sense," Dusty offered, "but what is the appropriate response when you identify these negative behaviors in the workforce?"

"Do you remember our conversation about the youngster who wasn't keen on eating his vegetables and how we framed the choices for him?"

"Of course!"

"Well, you frame the conversation with your team members in much the same way. First, you explain why certain behaviors are important: It is necessary to eat vegetables if you want to grow to be healthy. In your case, clarify that you are crafting a culture where you expect everyone to generate valucentricity. And in order to achieve such a cultural shift, living on purpose must be the rule.

"Next, you frame the choice in such a way that you express confidence in their ability to make good judgments: Which two vegetables would you like to eat? Or, for your team, how would you like to engage in order to accomplish our objectives in the most effective manner, while maintaining an environment of positivity? Then you let them make the choice. As long as the Key Performance Indicators are being met – eating vegetables with a good attitude – it doesn't really matter which vegetables they choose to eat, because you have only offered them healthy choices. Likewise in business, there are many methodologies that may be employed to accomplish the same objective. Allow latitude where you can, without compromising the outcomes. Let them own the choice and be responsible for the results.

"If they blatantly refuse to pursue value creation and positivity, or seek to negotiate unreasonably outside of the parameters, then you offer them another choice – one with well-stated consequences. Either they can buck against the established values and thereby choose to move in a different direction vocationally, *OR* they can seek to take *Ownership* and act in ways that support the organizational objectives and strengthen *Relationships*. Again, the choice is theirs and the options have been clearly delineated.

"So, you are establishing your values and making them clear. Then you are allowing everyone the opportunity to choose whether or not they will align their personal values with those of others within the organization. Is that correct?" Dusty asked.

"You've got it!" Fred responded. "People will begin to self-select. Of course, your hope is that everyone will choose to align with value creation and become invested in the outcomes. However, that's a bit idealistic. Not everyone will want to sail that ship. You quickly will be able to identify the *Victims, Naysayers,* and *Know-It-Alls*. Then, you can deal with them appropriately. And, deal with them you must. Their presence can be crippling.

"At this point, it is also important to note that leaders must be careful not to label people prematurely or inappropriately. Leaders must first ask themselves profound questions to become self-aware and make sure that they are leading well. Remember, honest self-evaluation is necessary to shift into growth gear. And, sometimes folks are resistant because leaders are simply leading poorly."

"How is that?" Dusty asked.

"Sometimes leaders move so quickly that they blow right past buy-in and start issuing edicts. I know that I have thrown a lot at you. But, if you will allow me, I would like to give you a formula that speaks to effecting positive change and getting everyone on board." Fred offered.

"I'm not overloaded yet. I think I can handle one more formula from my mechanic mentor," Dusty responded playfully.

"Good, I'm glad to know you still have a little bandwidth left," Fred retorted as he once again reached for a napkin. Notes on napkins had become standard protocol for their meetings.

"In the spirit of *We* over *Me*, there is another challenge I often lay before leaders. It has to do with making sure that they have broad-based buy-in, before they execute on their ideas or strategy. If leaders move too quickly toward implementation, without adequately garnering support, it can be perceived as a power play and create resistance in the ranks. Let me show you how this all plays out," Fred said as he wrote:

$$Q_i \times A = E$$

Then, he explained, "In this formula, the **Q_i** stands for *Quality idea*. It could be a product, a service, an initiative, or a dream for the future. The **A** represents the *Adoption* of that idea, which is a reflection of how well team members are aligned in their values and thinking. Where values are aligned, high levels of trust and respect exist. This high trust culture oils the gears, which must be engaged to produce movement toward a desired end or objective. The **E**, then, stands for *Execution* or the effective implementation of that *Quality idea*. If low levels of trust and lack of alignment mar a company's culture, then *Adoption* is hard to attain even if you have the best ideas in the world. Let me show you how this looks in practice.

"Let's say that another company has a world-class idea for a product. It ranks as a '10' on a scale of 1 to 10. It truly is a game-changing concept. However, imagine that the culture of that organization is weak and leaders are prone to push initiatives through. In that case, we might give them an *Adoption* rating of only 6. That would make their overall *Execution* score a 60 on a scale of 100. On the other hand, let's say you have a relatively good idea that might be rated an 8. By all objective measures, it is a slightly inferior offering. However, let's say that because of high trust, good leadership, shared values, and positivity, the culture of your organization provides an *Adoption* rating of 10. In this scenario, your overall *Execution* score is an impressive 80, which is to say that there is a 20 percent greater likelihood that your idea will be translated into reality and make it to market than that of the other company. That is the power of a healthy culture."

"That makes sense," Dusty offered. "I've seen a lot of great ideas fail simply because people weren't emotionally vested in the process."

"So have I," Fred added. "Sometimes I see leaders who are unwilling to seek advice or allow their ideas to be challenged or refined in the adoption process. They may feel that to compromise on the idea gives too much away, so they bulldoze through opposition and push their agendas. What they fail to realize is that the very act of mandating actually diminishes the impact of a quality idea, because you build emotional resistance. What might seem to be expeditious is, in reality, impeding the execution. Impatient leadership compromises the strength and momentum that could have been gained through valucentricity – aligning, unifying, and energizing the team.

"You see, it's often not the best product that wins in the market. Nor is it the brightest who seem to rise to the top of the corporate heap. Companies that thrive are resilient, tenacious and, most importantly, unified. Creative, innovative and adaptable are also adjectives used to describe **Remarkable!** organizations. But, unity is by far the most powerful force for good, and it's the result of a healthy culture. The best companies know that culture trumps everything else and they are intentional about crafting environments that are engaging and compelling. They don't leave culture to chance. It never happens by default. Culture is always by design in companies that are making a significant difference. Values are defined and they are aligned to cultivate a culture that is *Inspirational*. Does that make sense?" Fred asked as he concluded.

Unity is by far the most powerful force for good, and it's the result of a healthy culture.

"It makes perfectly good sense," said Dusty. "The impact of culture in any organization cannot be overstated. I can see now that culture is the single most important factor in the success of any organization and must be the highest priority of leadership. A company's culture is its greatest competitive advantage, and will either multiply a company's efforts, or divide both its performance and its people."

> **A company's culture is its greatest competitive advantage, and will either multiply a company's efforts, or divide both its performance and its people.**

"Correct," Fred responded. "The most important issue facing any business is to intentionally craft a **Remarkable!** *Culture* of value creation.' Everything else is secondary."

"You are going to have a culture," Dusty interjected, "because culture is simply the collective expression of the values, thoughts and behaviors of your people. The issue is whether your culture will be by design or default. Will intentional value creation be the force that crystallizes your culture? Or will you lean toward value extraction by default. And, will it be conspicuously unusual, delivering products and services that exceed all expectations? If you deliver extraordinary value, then people will talk about you. And when they talk about you, indeed you have become *Remarkable!*"

The most important issue facing any business is to intentionally craft a Remarkable! Culture of value creation.

"Stated with clarity and confidence," Fred affirmed. "In the process, valucentricity will serve to elevate engagement and improve morale, garnering discretionary effort from your team members. Now, one last thought I want you to consider."

"What's that?"

"The only way to help others learn and apply the Maxims of Value Creation is to embody them yourself. If you want them to impact your family, then it starts with you. If you are trying to transform the culture of an organization, then it has to start with you. You have to choose to start the process. You have to take the *OR* path. You must assume *Ownership* and make *Relationships* your highest priority. Mahatma Gandhi once said, 'Be the change you want to see in the world.' Change *around* you must always begin *within* you. The Superior Choice is about taking the initiative to create value.

Change around you must always begin within you. The Superior Choice is about taking the initiative to create value.

When Fred mentioned the Superior Choice, it reminded Dusty of what he had been carrying with him for weeks. He reached into his wallet and retrieved a napkin. He gently unfolded it and placed it on the table in front of them. On the napkin, Dusty had consolidated the growth spiral and the Value Creation formulas. Fred cracked a wry smile as he looked at the napkin.

After a moment, Fred turned the napkin over. On the other side, Dusty had written the *Clutch Question*. Once again, Fred took a pen from his pressed shirt pocket. He wrote a big 'P' in the center of the napkin, just below the *Question*.

"The P," he said, "stands for Pivotal Point. It is any clutch situation. It is the place where decisions are made that will begin a journey toward either *Alienation* or *Unity*. At each Pivotal Point, I can either choose to place the emphasis on *Us* or on *I*," Fred explained, as he wrote them on either side of the P. "If I choose to

```
        ↗
   ╭─────────────────╮
  ( Unity / inspiration )
   ╰─────────────────╯
   ╭─────────────────╮
  ( Solution – orientation )
   ╰─────────────────╯
   ╭─────────────────╮
  ( Honest Evaluation )
   ╰─────────────────╯
```

$VE =$ ‖ Clutch Situation ‖ $VC =$
$I/Us \times ER$ $We/Me \times OR$

```
   ╭─────────────────╮
  ( Rationalization )
   ╰─────────────────╯
   ╭─────────────────╮
  ( Stagnation )
   ╰─────────────────╯
   ╭─────────────────────╮
  ( Alienation / Desperation )
   ╰─────────────────────╯
        ↙
```

put *We* over *Me*, then I have chosen to emphasize *Us* and will seek to create value for *Us*. On the other hand, if I place *Me* over *We*, then I seek to extract value and make choices that will disengage the growth gear and start a descent down the spiral. Again, it's a choice.

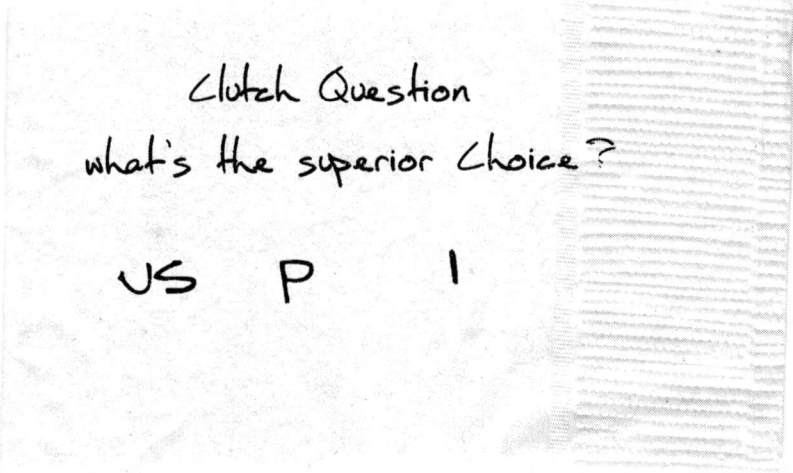

"Living on purpose means that the choice is always in my hands. *I* have to choose whether *I* will pursue the *ER* or the *OR* path in life. The *ER* is about *Ego* and *Rivalry* against others – positioning myself to extract value. While *OR* is about taking *Ownership* and highly valuing *Relationships*. Notice that the first person pronoun '*I*' always stands in the middle of that choice, because *I* alone can make that decision. *I* cannot expect others to move first. *I* must take the initiative in the process of value creation. *I* must act responsibly in making the Superior Choice to create value." Fred wrote on the napkin again.

> Clutch Question
> what's the superior Choice?
>
> US P ER I OR

Dusty looked for a moment at what Fred had written on the napkin. In a flash of insight it all came together. Like staring into a hologram and seeing the third dimension pop off of the page, the elements of the Superior Choice were all right there before his eyes.

With excitement in his voice, Dusty began to recap what he heard Fred say. "The P represents the Pivotal Point, which is any clutch situation. On one side of the P is *Us* and on the other is *I*, representing the choice to either create or extract value. The *I* also stands for personal responsibility to choose between either *ER* or *OR*. Flip the *Us* and bring it all together and you have all the ingredients necessary to make the *SUPERIOR Choice!*"

Dusty took the pen that Fred had placed on the table and wrote on the napkin:

> Clutch Question
> what's the superior Choice?
>
> US P ER I OR
>
> SUPERIOR

"I really think you've got it," Fred said as he beamed his smile from ear to ear. "You see, you set yourself up to become **Remarkable!** when you take the time to ask the *Clutch Question: What is the Superior Choice?* It forces you to tap into the core of who you are and draw strength from those things that you value the most. It allows you to act consistently with what you hold in highest regard and prevents you from becoming a prisoner of your self-protective devices and knee-jerk reactions. In other words, you *live on purpose* and act in a way that rises above the circumstances. You actually create value by design while you live intentionally. And, when you act in ways that defy what others expect – you seek to continuously *create value* rather than *extract value* – then people take notice and begin to remark about it. Those remarks invariably create a buzz about you and your business. People will be talking both inside and outside the business about how conspicuously unusual you are in a marketplace filled with people who are seeking merely to *extract value*. And when others begin to describe you as extraordinary, then indeed you have become **Remarkable!**

The impact of culture in any organization cannot be overstated. The culture is the single most important factor in the success of any organization and must be the highest priority of leadership.

Chapter Sixteen

Reward

I n Dusty's reading, he ran across a quote that reminded him of Fred's challenge to always take the initiative in value creation. He had it framed and hung in his office to remind him of where transformation must always begin. A monk wrote it anonymously centuries ago, but the truths it contains are timeless. It reads:

I Wanted to Change the World
When I was a young man, I wanted to change the world.
I found it was difficult to change the world,
so I tried to change my nation.

*When I found I couldn't change the nation,
I began to focus on my town. I couldn't change the town,
so as an older man, I tried to change my family.*

*As an old man, I have come to realize that the only thing
I can change is me. Now, I understand that if long ago
I had changed myself, I could have made an impact on my
family.*

*My family and I could have made an impact on our town.
The influence of our town could have helped shape the nation,
and thereby I could have changed the world.*

Change at Query came slowly and steadily at first. The Maxims of Value Creation were becoming consciously grafted into the culture of the organization. Leaders were constantly challenged to embody them. They guided team meetings. New associates were encouraged to embrace them as a part of the on-boarding process. Conversations throughout the organization were peppered with the language of value creation and positivity. The mission statement was made ever-present and modified to read:

"Creating Value for Everyone We Encounter."

And, it wasn't merely the text of the mission statement that had changed. Associates at Query no longer simply *had a mission*. They were *on a mission!* And the difference was **Remarkable!** One department took the initiative to produce and distribute rubber wristbands. They were engraved with the words *CREATE VALUE*, reminding everyone to stay on the *OR* side and shift into growth gear in order to generate valucentricity. Best practices, which had once been hoarded as competitive advantages over other business units, were shared freely. Friendly competition, which once subtly created silos within the organization, was replaced by collaboration and a new spirit of collegiality was fostered. Associates began to show up voluntarily for work a little earlier during heavy work cycles and stay a little later when deadlines were approaching.

At the same time, if team members put too much time on the clock, leadership noticed it and encouraged them to make sure that they were spending appropriate time creating value at home, with those that mattered most. Organizational health seemed to follow personal health. When people's personal lives were better, they brought a better self to work and productivity increased.

It took several months before the metrics moved in a positive direction. It took time for the concepts of value creation to take root, but when they did they began to spread like bluebonnets across Texas in spring. An attitude of positivity eventually swallowed up the pockets of negativity. *Naysayers* and *Victims* were either converted or called out. *Know-It-Alls* were marginalized.

Dusty knew that they were on the right track. He could sense and see a new spirit emerging. Team members felt empowered, as they were encouraged to maximize their strengths and passion to solve problems. Associates were talking about how they could create movements of good for their clients and for one another. A swell of hope and optimism significantly raised the energy level within the office. And positive signs were being seen in the customer satisfaction scores as advisors dedicated themselves to taking ownership of customer relationships and responsibility for providing quick resolution to issues raised by those clients. A buzz was being created about the organization – both internally and externally. Team members were talking openly about how proud they were to be a part of the vision and the mission of Query. At the same time, they were experiencing a significant uptick in referrals. The word that was often used to describe the change that was taking place was **_Remarkable!_** But, the changes that got Dusty most excited were taking place at home.

Dusty had been making a conscientious effort to be less critical of Mike. He quit offering his unsolicited advice and tried hard to curtail his need to control his son's every move. Instead, Dusty started looking for ways to encourage Mike to explore the options before him, owning his decision-making processes and taking what he felt was the appropriate action. Mike began to feel empowered as Dusty exercised less control over his life.

Consequently, Mike gave more thoughtful consideration to his choices, knowing that the consequences would be fully his to face. Even though Dusty still felt the need to make it clear that he would not rescue Mike from the consequences of poor choices, it was an unnecessary warning. Mike began demonstrating maturity and discernment in most all of his decisions. He started taking more initiative in his schoolwork and completed chores around the house before being asked. What Dusty had long interpreted as laziness, he now realized was nothing more than Mike's way of expressing his frustration over feeling powerless to make his own decisions.

For the first time in a long time, Mike began to initiate conversations with Dusty. Once he stopped offering his fatherly counsel without invitation, Mike actually started asking for Dusty's advice. Rather than pontificating, Dusty was learning to ask thoughtful questions, allowing Mike to extrapolate an issue to its logical conclusion and then make a choice that he could own. Debates were replaced with meaningful discussions about Mike's hopes, dreams and aspirations. The wall of defensiveness that had been built between them was being dismantled brick by emotional brick. It was happening gradually, but resentment was giving way to mutual respect.

For the first time that Dusty could ever remember, he began to believe the best in Mike rather than question his every motive. Trust was being restored. After awhile they actually started to enjoy each other's company again. As a result, they worked together to plan trips to two college campuses – schools of Mike's choosing. And, best of all, they both looked forward to spending the time together discussing the options for Mike's future.

The biggest changes, however, were taking place in his relationship with Lisa. The tone of their interactions immediately began to change when Dusty started applying the principles of value creation and making Superior Choices in their relationship. For years he had attempted to get his needs met by extracting value from their relationship rather than seeking to bring value to it. Now, his attitude had been radically altered. Rather than demanding or seeking to manipulate Lisa into meeting his needs, he started asking questions about how he could enrich their relationship. And, he listened intently to her answers.

He began to anticipate her needs and sought to bring the greatest value to every conversation and situation. He began to think and act in ways that had Lisa's best interest at heart. Rather than finding fault in her, he became more conscious of his own shortcomings. This new self-awareness began to cultivate within him an attitude of humility. But with that humility came a confidence like nothing he had experienced before, because he knew he was leading by example for the first time in their lives together. Rather than being threatened by the knowledge of his weaknesses, he was emboldened to keep himself in growth gear.

Dusty was inspired to invest in his relationship with Lisa in new ways. For years he had sought to advance his skill sets for the sake of advancing his career. Now he was seeking every means possible to advance their marriage. He read books, registered the two of them for a marriage conference and put a date night on the calendar each week so they could be alone and have meaningful conversations.

At first, Lisa was skeptical of Dusty's intentions and frankly a bit confused. She wondered what aliens had abducted her husband and had left this foreign being to replace him. Though he tried to explain to her all that he had learned about value creation, he was much more effective in doing so at the office than he was at home. Her cool response to his enthusiasm often left Dusty frustrated, but he tried his best to be patient. Rather than try to explain, he made a personal commitment to live on purpose and lead by example. He was choosing to continue to create value in their relationship regardless of her response.

When Lisa became angry or expressed disappointment, he fought back his natural tendency to rationalize his behavior. Instead, he chose to be open and humble, avoiding the slippery slope toward alienation. He stayed fully engaged in each situation and conversation, evaluating the options, and seeking a solution that would inspire them both to become better. And, in those moments when he slipped back into old patterns, he was quick to own his actions and apologize before he defaulted into a defensive position, escalating the situation and making matters worse.

To moderate his expectations, Dusty convinced himself that it was going to take quite a while for Lisa to work through the broken trust issues that had built a barrier between them. It was only reasonable to think it would take time to get back to a place where they could once again confide in each other. He had made a commitment to himself that he would strive to demonstrate extraordinary patience during this period of healing. He was surprised, however, by how soon Lisa started to soften once she saw a noticeable change in his attitude and demeanor toward her. It didn't happen overnight, but she slowly began to feel safe in his presence again.

For the first time in a long time, she no longer felt that she had to fight to protect herself. Fear and trepidation gradually yielded to openness and curiosity. Trust was being restored one encounter at a time. She was beginning to feel as if she had found a long-lost friend. A transformation of a personal nature was taking place – one Dusty could have neither orchestrated nor dictated.

As for Dusty, he was content with incremental progress and was actually enjoying the opportunity to court his wife again. He knew that they had much to rebuild and that it would be a lifelong process. But that was all right with him, because now he knew that he wanted to spend the rest of his life with Lisa and he felt confident that he was on the right track. His heart had experienced a cataclysmic shift. He really wanted the marriage to work and was willing to invest whatever time and energy necessary to woo back the bride of his youth. He was all in. The more he focused on the *We* and creating value, the more he saw Lisa soften. He was confident that with enough time and consistency Lisa would be able to climb out of her protective tower and join him in the process.

Life had changed dramatically for Dusty since Fred first gave him a ride home the night his car's clutch had failed. The idea of a "clutch" had taken on a whole new meaning. Now he saw every interpersonal encounter as a *clutch situation* – an opportunity to engage with others in a transformational way. He now asked himself the *Clutch Question* at every pivotal point, which allowed Dusty to make the Superior Choice and move toward value creation. His decisions were now framed within the context of *We* over *Me* thinking, and the *OR Factor* multiplied his efforts. He not only began to inspire those around him, but he actually began to inspire himself. Dusty no longer felt helpless and desperate. He no longer felt the need to control those around him. He was in control of himself.

He allowed others to exert their freedom of choice without feeling the need to dictate. He was growing to be an exemplary leader, and he was enjoying the contentment he felt – both at work and at home. Dusty was empowered by the confidence that his choices could have a positive impact on his corner of the world. Consequently, broken relationships were being restored. Life was marked with less conflict and more unity. He no longer felt the need to compete with others in a feeble attempt to prove his value. Seeking collaboration in every *clutch situation* opened new worlds of possibilities. For the first time in his life, Dusty felt at peace with himself and the world. He was living for something much bigger than himself. He was *living on purpose*. And, he was experiencing valucentricity. Life was good.

The changes that Dusty had experienced since his first conversation with Fred at the coffee shop truly were **Remarkable!** His perspective on life had shifted significantly since he had discovered and started applying the Maxims of Value Creation. And he wasn't the only one who was being positively impacted. By taking the initiative and making the choice to create and bring more value to every encounter and endeavor, those closest to him were beginning to take notice and talk about how things somehow seemed to be changing for the good.

And, Dusty knew in his heart of hearts that if the principles he had learned over the course of the past few months could have such a profoundly positive impact on his closest relationships, he was confident that they would continue to create a better culture at work as well. It was all about making better choices – Superior Choices – that possess the power to unify a diverse workforce by focusing on value creation and personal responsibility. It all seemed so simple, yet it was so profound. By making better choices, Dusty was creating a better life for himself, his family and for the organization. He no longer had a problem with his clutch. In fact, Dusty had become a clutch player – standing in the gap and offering peak performance under pressure.

On the work front, the principles of value creation had an unexpected impact. The concept of value engineering had taken on a whole new meaning. Rather than just trying to engineer costs out of their offerings at Query, they began to look for ways to engineer more client value into each offering. Value was now defined by the experience, not just the expense. As they provided more value, clients less frequently questioned their pricing structure. As a matter of fact, Query made it abundantly clear that they were not the lowest-cost provider in their space. They actually began to take pride in the fact that they no longer used lowballing as a sales strategy and loss leaders became a notion of the past. Instead, they offered unexpected value for the price. As a trusted partner, they were becoming known for delivering extraordinary service that went above and beyond expectations. And as a result, people were beginning to talk about their remarkable customer service experiences.

In the midst of this metamorphosis, Dusty was reaffirmed in his belief that the culture of any organization was its only real advantage – the Superior Advantage – in the marketplace. A truly differentiating culture is one that is characterized by empowerment and value creation. It is a culture where values are aligned, thinking is enhanced and behaviors are inspired to achieve superior results. This **Remarkable!** *Culture* produces an environment where silos are shattered and synergy prevails. In such a setting, movements of good have the potential to produce exponential returns, reducing competition and amplifying collaboration. Loyalty, morale and discretionary effort are all actualized as by-products of value creation. Cultures where people BELIEVE the best *IN* each other; WANT the best *FOR* each other; and, EXPECT the best *FROM* each other are conspicuously unusual. When you experience them, you can immediately *tell* that they are different. And people are compelled to remark about them both internally and externally. This kind of culture invariably creates a buzz about your business.

Dusty also understood that creating this kind of culture –

whether in a family or a multi-national corporation – all begins with a personal choice. And Dusty had committed himself to be intentional about crafting a **Remarkable!** *Culture* in each corner of his world – one choice at a time. He had discovered the simple truth that in every *clutch situation* each one of us has a choice to make: We either *extract value from OR create value for* those within our sphere of influence. And, if we choose to *create value,* the results can be truly **Remarkable!**

APPENDICES

APPENDIX A

How to Use *Remarkable!*

Cultural Transformation

Many organizations are depleted daily by a number of associates who are seeking to *extract value from* their endeavors rather than seeking to *create and bring value to* the work environment. The four Maxims of Value Creation introduced in **Remarkable!** can be leveraged through corporate book clubs, team meetings, onboarding processes or in a lunch-n-learn setting to discuss how these principles may be applied to breed unity and create an atmosphere where people are encouraged to use their gifts and pursue their passion for the purpose of solving problems and creating a culture of positivity.

Foundational Text

Remarkable! can be used as a textbook in university and business school courses. The content can enhance courses on leadership, ethics, business management and organizational health. The content can complement the competency and skill set development that is often central in academic life. The content in **Remarkable!** offers a good balance between principles that enhance competency and principles that will increase emotional intelligence.

Corporate Retreats and Speaking Engagements

Invite us to invest in your teams. We work with clients to enhance corporate retreats, customer forums, high potential training programs, and industry keynote presentations.

For more information. Please visit us at:

www.CreateRemarkable.com

APPENDIX B

Assess Yourself...

The Judgment Index

Explore the concepts from **Remarkable!** for you and your team using *The Judgment Index*™. *The Judgment Index* provides real, quantifiable insight into a person's judgment capacity and decision-making capabilities. *The Judgment Index* is one of the most scientific, mathematical, and logically based assessment tools in the market. No other assessment tool available today provides such a unique perspective on measuring judgment – and its underlying valuation construct. This extensive report reveals ways to enhance your performance and gain deeper levels of satisfaction and fulfillment.

The Engagement Index

Identifying and quantifying twelve foundational factors that drive performance, this instrument provides insight and helpful narrative to assist individuals in managing their "emotional energy levels." A thin-slice of the complete *Judgment Index*, the *Engagement Index* provides useful coaching fodder to produce improved organizational performance. Assessing the emotional "will" and addressing the appropriate issues will significantly enhance the deployment of your "skill" in any endeavor.

To complete either assessment, visit us at:
http://CreateRemarkable.com/assessments/

Selection and Hiring

Remarkable! can also provide your organization with a wide array of value-based, selection assessments, to ensure that you are "getting the right people on the bus and in the right seats." A *Remarkable Culture* begins by getting the right people onboard and coaching them to success. Contact us for more detailed information on how we can enhance your hiring processes.

For more information, vist:
http://CreateRemarkable.com/HireWell/

APPENDIX C

Remarkable! Culture Survey

Read each statement below and provide the score that most accurately reflects your beliefs regarding the organization in the space provided to the left. Rank your responses on a scale from 1 to 10, with 1 = strongly disagree; 10 = strongly agree.

_____ 1. Everyone within the organization can clearly articulate our values and our mission is clear and inspirational.

_____ 2. We all embody (live out) the values of the organization. Our "walk matches our talk."

_____ 3. Team members believe that what we do as a company impacts people's lives in a positive way.

_____ 4. We use tools and processes to select and hire team members who share our values.

_____ 5. Leaders seek a high level of buy-in from team members before implementing initiatives.

_____ 6. Cooperation and collaboration are actively encouraged and win-win resolutions are pursued.

_____ 7. Authority is delegated so that people can act responsibly to fulfill corporate objectives.

_____ 8. There is a high level of trust throughout the organization. People *believe the best in each other, want the best for each other* and *expect the best from each other.*

_____ 9. Expectations are made clear and people are held accountable for the work that they produce.

_____ 10. The organization invests heavily in developing team members and learning is an important objective in our day-to-day work.

_____ Total of scores

Rating:

90+   The culture of the organization is healthy and you could be described as **Remarkable!**

80-90   Although this is a fairly good score, there is room for improvement. Intentional work could produce exponential returns.

70-80   An average score; lackluster performance and low engagement prevail.

<70   Unhealthy symptoms exist within the organization, greatly inhibiting performance.

APPENDIX D

Robert S. Hartman

A Tribute

Robert S. Hartman, PhD, was born in Berlin, Germany on January 27, 1910. A brilliant and energetic person, he studied at the German College of Political Science, the University of Paris (La Sorbonne), the London School of Economics, and Berlin University. By the age of 22 he had earned his law degree and began to teach at Berlin University, while also working as an assistant district court judge.

In the early stages of his career, Hartman's life would change forever. He was witness to the emerging Hitler "system." In Hitler he saw a man who was not only evil, but also a man who was able to organize evil. Hartman openly opposed and spoke out against Hitler and all that he represented. Evading many brushes with death, Hartman faced constant danger. He was able to escape to England on a falsified passport just as the Nazis closed in on him. In England, he was hired by the Walt Disney Corporation to strategize and help them open the company in parts of Europe and South America. Hartman quickly rose through the Disney ranks, even serving as Walt Disney's personal advisor.

However, Hartman was continually haunted by the idea that Hitler had learned how to organize evil. If that was possible, would it also be possible to organize goodness? He spent the rest of his life in the pursuit of an answer to that question. The quest led him to leave Disney and begin his studies and research in the field of axiology – the science of value. His work in axiology established the relationship of values to judgment. As his work relates to business, he was referring to excellence and quality outcomes.

It was this thinking that led him to construct the Hartman Value Profile – a tool that has been called one of the most mathematical, scientific, and logically-based assessment instruments ever created. Dr. Stephen Byrum's personal work with Dr. Hartman, along with four decades of assessment interpretations and experience with the Value Profile, is the foundation for the Judgment Index™.

Hartman spent the rest his life researching, writing, lecturing and teaching. He earned his PhD at Northwestern University in 1946 and taught throughout the United States, Canada, Latin America, and Europe. Hartman taught at Ohio State University, Massachusetts Institute of Technology (MIT) and Yale University. Dr. Hartman was a former research professor at the University of Tennessee and the National University of Mexico. Known as the "father of modern axiology," Hartman authored more than ten books and over 100 articles. Before his untimely death in 1973, Robert S. Hartman's work was nominated for the Nobel Prize for his promotion of human self-understanding, the advancement of the most important human values, and the implications of his work for transforming life in the most positive ways.

For more information, visit: **www.HartmanInstitute.org**

APPENDIX E

Glossary of Terms

Abundance Mentality – the belief that by collaborating to *create value* there can be an abundance of resources produced that may be shared by those who were involved in the creative process.

Axiology – the study of values, value constructs and value creation and their subsequent impact on a person's thoughts, beliefs, decision-making processes and performance.

Clutch Situation – any situation that requires two or more parties to work together; providing an opportunity for the engagement of two or more components to create forward progress.

Cultural Transformation Formula –
Value Alignment > $\triangle$ thinking > $\triangle$ behaviors = $\triangle$ Results.

Culture – the collective expression of the values, thinking and behaviors that individuals bring to the organization.

Living on Purpose – values-based, intentional living; Living on purpose means you live purposefully, with purpose, and for a purpose.

Remarkable - notably or conspicuously unusual; extraordinary; Worthy of notice or attention.

Scarcity Mentality – the belief that there are only limited resources in the world and that in order to survive one must deprive someone else of those resources; this perspective on life causes people to compete to *extract value* in each situation to insure survival.

Superior – higher in station, rank, degree or importance; above the average in excellence, merit or intelligence; of higher grade or quality.

Valucentricity – the energy and momentum that is produced when values are properly identified and aligned; producing a unified and energized work force.

Value Creation Equation – VC = We/Me x *OR*

Value Extraction Equation – VE = I/Us x *ER*

Value Grade – the value that a person *creates for* and *brings to* the organization or endeavor; as opposed to pay grade – which speaks to the value that someone *extracts from* the organization. When your value grade exceeds your pay grade, then you become invaluable to the organization – if not indispensable.

APPENDIX F

The Maxims of Value Creation

The Maxim of Creativity
We are designed to create value in life.

The Maxim of Positivity
Authentic positivity is the by-product of creating true value.

The Maxim of Sustainability
To continuously create value, leverage your passion and strengths to solve problems.

The Maxim of Responsibility
Ownership empowers people to take responsibility for creating value.

Bibliography

Arbinger Institute. *Leadership and Self-Deception*. San Francisco: Berrett-Koehler Publishers, 2010.

Byrum, C. Stephen and Leland Kaiser. *Spirit for Greatness: Spiritual Dimensions of Organizations and Their Leadership*. Littleton, MA: Tapestry Press, Ltd, 2004.

Byrum, C. Stephen. *From the Neck Up: The Recovery and Sustaining of the Human Element in Modern Organizations*. Littleton, MA: Tapestry Press, Ltd, 2006.

Buckingham, Marcus and Donald O. Clifton. *Now, Discover Your Strengths*. New York: The Free Press, 2001

Cathy, S. Truett. *It's Easier to Succeed than to Fail*. Nashville: Thomas Nelson, 1989.

Collins, Jim. *Good to Great*. New York: HarperCollins, 2001.

Covey, Stephen M.R. *The Speed of Trust*. New York: The Free Press, 2008.

DeLong, Thomas J. and Sara DeLong. "Managing Yourself: The Paradox of Excellence." *Harvard Business Review* (June 8, 2011): 7-20.

Demarist, Peter D. and Harvey J. Schoof. *Answering the Central Question: How Science Reveals the Keys to Success in Life, Love, and Leadership*. Heartlead Publishing, 2010.

Frankl, Viktor. *Man's Search for Meaning*. Boston: Beacon Press, 2006

Frankl, Viktor. *Man's Search for Ultimate Meaning*. New York: Basic Books, 2000.

Hartman, Robert S. *The Structure of Value*. Carbondale, IL: Southern Illinois University Press, 1969.

Herrmann, Robert L. *Sir John Templeton: Supporting Scientific Research for Spiritual Discoveries*. Philadelphia: Templeton Press, 2004.

Milne, A. A. *Winnie The Pooh*. Boston: Dutton Juvenile, 1996.

Pomeroy, Leon. *The New Science of Axiological Psychology*. New York: Rodopi, 2005.

Sanders, Tim. *Love is the Killer App*. New York: Three Rivers Press, 2002.

Seligman, Martin E. P. *Learned Optimism*. New York: Vantage Books, 2006.

Stanley, Andy. *The Principle of the Path*. Nashville: Thomas Nelson, 2011.

Acknowledgements

Acknowledgement seems like such a feeble way to express the immense gratitude that we hold for those who have supported us in this project. Any success this book may experience will be due to our "tribe" of friends, who have served as mentors, cheerleaders, and fans. It would be impossible to mention them all, but we would be remiss in not thanking a few. So it is with deep gratitude and humility that we would like to express our appreciation to the following folks for their contributions:

Our countless friends, family members and associates who have encouraged us to put our thoughts on paper so that others may benefit from lessons we have learned through life experience and by "going to school" on some ***Remarkable!*** companies.

To LuAnne and Lynn, our wives, for giving us more "hall passes" than we deserve.

S. Truett Cathy and the entire Cathy family. Through their faithfulness to these principles, a corporate culture has been created at Chick-fil-A that has served to inspire many.

Acknowledgements

David Stockert and Peter Bourke for being bold in their feedback on the early iterations of the content. Without their insightful comments and candor, this project would have been convoluted.

Randy Walton and Dana McArthur for their efforts in keeping the content "sticky" and making sure that it is delivered in an engaging way. We anxiously await your completion of *The Guide to Becoming **Remarkable!***

Kay Acton, Anne Alexander and Carolyn Zauche. Without their editorial prowess, this project would have been replete with split infinitives, misspelled words and misplaced commas. Thanks for your eagle eyes and mastery of the English language.

Pat Malone for his patience, determination and creativity in producing a ***Remarkable!*** cover and book design.

Tara Ashley for keeping us organized and making sure that the communication on this project was not bottlenecked by our busy schedules.

About the Authors

Dr. Randy Ross

Dr. Randy Ross is founder and CEO (Chief Enthusiasm Officer) of **Remarkable!**, a corporate advisory and consulting firm specializing in talent selection instruments, cultural development and organizational health. Randy is a "craftsman of culture and a catalytic coach," whose purpose is to see others inspired and excelling in all aspects of life. Utilizing the same value-based diagnostic and developmental instruments described in this book, **Remarkable!** helps companies craft cultures of Value Creation.

Spending time in both the for-profit and not-for-profit worlds, he has traveled throughout the United States and internationally as a speaker, consultant and coach, building teams and developing leaders. A compelling communicator, Dr. Ross has the keen sensitivity to speak to the heart of leaders and inspires elevated performance among teams.

For more information visit: **CreateRemarkable.com**

David Salyers

David Salyers has been on quite a journey. Having graduated from college on a Saturday morning, he started his career with Chick-fil-A before the day was over. Currently serving as the Vice President of National, Regional and Local Marketing for Chick-fil-A, Inc., David has invested his entire career as part of a team, committed to building the kind of company culture that people talk about!

As a passionate student of life and business, he has spent over thirty years seeing the principles in this book play out corporately and in over 1,600 Chick-fil-A restaurants across the country. Serving as a board member for numerous non-profit organizations, and a few for-profit startups, has convinced him further that the principles contained within these pages are universally applicable. Having the unique opportunity to witness both great leaders and great organizations, he is energized to pass along the principles he has discovered from a personal journey, which can only be described as...**Remarkable!**

CPSIA information can be obtained at www.ICGtesting.com
Printed in the USA
LVOW06*0140210813

348885LV00003B/5/P